Stories of Ir

Rebecca Harding Davis et al.

Alpha Editions

This edition published in 2024

ISBN : 9789362925688

Design and Setting By
Alpha Editions
www.alphaedis.com
Email - info@alphaedis.com

Contents

THE HOUSE AND THE BRAIN.
BY E. BULWER LYTTON.

A FRIEND of mine, who is a man of letters and a philosopher, said to me one day, as if between jest and earnest, "Fancy! since we last met I have discovered a haunted house in the midst of London."

"Really haunted? and by what,—ghosts?"

"Well, I can't answer these questions; all I know is this: six weeks ago I and my wife were in search of a furnished apartment. Passing a quiet street, we saw on the window of one of the houses a bill, 'Apartments Furnished.' The situation suited us; we entered the house, liked the rooms, engaged them by the week, and left them the third day. No power on earth could have reconciled my wife to stay longer; and I don't wonder at it."

"What did you see?"

"Excuse me; I have no desire to be ridiculed as a superstitious dreamer, nor, on the other hand, could I ask you to accept on my affirmation what you would hold to be incredible, without the evidence of your own senses. Let me only say this: it was not so much what we saw or heard (in which you might fairly suppose that we were the dupes of our own excited fancy, or the victims of imposture in others) that drove us away, as it was an undefinable terror which seized both of us whenever we passed by the door of a certain unfurnished room, in which we neither saw nor heard anything; and the strangest marvel of all was, that for once in my life I agreed with my wife, silly woman though she be, and allowed after the third night that it was impossible to stay a fourth in that house. Accordingly, on the fourth morning I summoned the woman who kept the house and attended on us, and told her that the rooms did not quite suit us, and we would not stay out our week. She said dryly, 'I know why; you have stayed longer than any other lodger. Few ever stayed a second night; none before you a third. But I take it they have been very kind to you.'

"'They,—who?' I asked, affecting a smile.

"'Why, they who haunt the house, whoever they are; I don't mind them; I remember them many years ago, when I lived in this house not as a servant; but I know they will be the death of me some day. I don't care,—I'm old and must die soon anyhow; and then I shall be with them, and in this house still.' The woman spoke with so dreary a calmness, that really it was a sort of awe that prevented my conversing with her further. I paid for my week, and too happy were I and my wife to get off so cheaply."

"You excite my curiosity," said I; "nothing I should like better than to sleep in a haunted house. Pray give me the address of the one which you left so ignominiously."

My friend gave me the address; and when we parted I walked straight toward the house thus indicated.

It is situated on the north side of Oxford Street, in a dull but respectable thoroughfare. I found the house shut up; no bill at the window, and no response to my knock. As I was turning away, a beer-boy, collecting pewter pots at the neighboring areas, said to me, "Do you want any one at that house, sir?"

"Yes, I heard it was to be let."

"Let! Why, the woman who kept it is dead; has been dead these three weeks; and no one can be found to stay there, though Mr. J—— offered ever so much. He offered mother, who chars for him, £1 a week just to open and shut the windows, and she would not."

"Would not! and why?"

"The house is haunted; and the old woman who kept it was found dead in her bed with her eyes wide open. They say the Devil strangled her."

"Pooh! You speak of Mr. J——. Is he the owner of the house?"

"Yes."

"Where does he live?"

"In G—— Street, No.—."

"What is he?—in any business?"

"No, sir; nothing particular; a single gentleman."

I gave the pot-boy the gratuity earned by his liberal information, and proceeded to Mr. J—— in G—— Street, which was close by the street that boasted the haunted house. I was lucky enough to find Mr. J—— at home; an elderly man with intelligent countenance and prepossessing manners.

I communicated my name and my business frankly. I said I heard the house was considered to be haunted; that I had a strong desire to examine a house with so equivocal a reputation; that I should be greatly obliged if he would allow me to hire it, though only for a night. I was willing to pay for that privilege whatever he might be inclined to ask. "Sir," said Mr. J—— with great courtesy, "the house is at your service for as short or as long a time as you please. Rent is out of the question; the obligation will be on my side, should you be able to discover the cause of the strange phenomena which at present deprive it of all value. I cannot let it, for I cannot even get a servant to keep it in order or answer the door. Unluckily, the house is haunted, if I may use that expression, not only by night but by day; though at night the disturbances are of a more unpleasant and sometimes of a more alarming character. The poor old woman who died in it three weeks ago was a pauper whom I took out of a workhouse; for in her childhood she had been known to some of my family, and had once been in such good circumstances that she had rented that house of my uncle. She was a woman of superior education and strong mind, and was the only person I could ever induce to remain in the house. Indeed, since her death, which was sudden, and the coroner's inquest, which gave it a notoriety in the neighborhood, I have so despaired of finding any person to take charge of it, much more a tenant, that I would willingly let it rent free for a year to any one who would pay its rates and taxes."

"How long ago did the house acquire this character?"

"That I can scarcely tell you, but many years since; the old woman I spoke of said it was haunted when she rented it, between thirty and forty years ago. The fact is, that my life has been spent in the East Indies, and in the civil service of the company. I returned to England last year, on inheriting the fortune of an uncle, amongst whose possessions was the house in question. I found it shut up and uninhabited. I was told that it was haunted, and no one would inhabit it. I smiled at what seemed to me so idle a story. I spent some money in repainting and roofing it, added to its old-fashioned furniture a few modern articles, advertised it, and obtained a lodger for a year. He was a colonel retired on half pay. He came in with his family, a son and a daughter, and four or five servants; they all left the house the next day; and although they deponed that they had all seen something different, that something was equally terrible to all. I really could not in conscience sue, or even blame, the colonel for breach of agreement. Then I put in the old woman I have spoken of, and she was empowered to let the house in apartments. I never had one lodger who stayed more than three days. I do not tell you their stories; to no two lodgers have exactly the same phenomena been repeated. It is better that you should judge for yourself, than enter the house with an imagination influenced by previous narratives; only be prepared to see and to hear something or other, and take whatever precautions you yourself please."

"Have you never had a curiosity yourself to pass a night in that house?"

"Yes; I passed, not a night, but three hours in broad daylight alone in that house. My curiosity is not satisfied, but it is quenched. I have no desire to renew the experiment. You cannot complain, you see, sir, that I am not sufficiently candid; and unless your interest be exceedingly eager and your nerves unusually strong, I honestly add that I advise you *not* to pass a night in that house."

"My interest *is* exceedingly keen," said I; "and though only a coward will boast of his nerves in situations wholly unfamiliar to him, yet my nerves have been seasoned in such variety of danger that I have the right to rely on them, even in a haunted house."

Mr. J—— said very little more; he took the keys of the house out of his bureau, and gave them to me; and, thanking him cordially for his frankness and his urbane concession to my wish, I carried off my prize.

Impatient for the experiment, as soon as I reached home I summoned my confidential servant,—a young man of gay spirits, fearless temper, and as free from superstitious prejudice as any one I could think of.

"F——," said I, "you remember in Germany how disappointed we were at not finding a ghost in that old castle, which was said to be haunted by a headless apparition? Well, I have heard of a house in London which, I have reason to hope, is decidedly haunted. I mean to sleep there to-night. From what I hear, there is no doubt that something will allow itself to be seen or to be heard,—something perhaps excessively horrible. Do you think, if I take you with me, I may rely on your presence of mind, whatever may happen?"

"O sir! pray trust me!" said he, grinning with delight.

"Very well, then, here are the keys of the house; this is the address. Go now, select for me any bedroom you please; and since the house has not been inhabited for weeks, make up a good fire, air the bed well, see, of course, that there are candles as well as fuel. Take with you my revolver and my dagger,—so much for my weapons,—arm yourself equally well; and if we are not a match for a dozen ghosts, we shall be but a sorry couple of Englishmen."

I was engaged for the rest of the day on business so urgent that I had not leisure to think much on the nocturnal adventure to which I had plighted my honor. I dined alone and very late, and while dining read, as is my habit. The volume I selected was one of Macaulay's essays. I thought to myself that I would take the book with me; there was so much of healthfulness in the style, and practical life in the subjects, that it would serve as an antidote against the influences of superstitious fancy.

Accordingly, about half past nine, I put the book into my pocket, and strolled leisurely towards the haunted house. I took with me a favorite dog; an exceedingly sharp, bold, and vigilant bull-terrier, a dog fond of prowling about strange ghostly corners and passages at night in search of rats, a dog of dogs for a ghost.

It was a summer night, but chilly, the sky somewhat gloomy and overcast; still there was a moon,—faint and sickly, but still a moon; and if the clouds permitted, after midnight it would be brighter.

I reached the house, knocked, and my servant opened with a cheerful smile.

"All right, sir, and very comfortable."

"Oh!" said I, rather disappointed; "have you not seen nor heard anything remarkable?"

"Well, sir, I must own I have heard something queer."

"What?—what?"

"The sound of feet pattering behind me; and once or twice small noises like whispers close at my ear; nothing more."

"You are not at all frightened?"

"I! not a bit of it, sir!" And the man's bold look reassured me on one point, namely, that, happen what might, he would not desert me.

We were in the hall, the street door closed, and my attention was now drawn to my dog. He had at first run in eagerly enough, but had sneaked back to the door, and was scratching and whining to get out. After I had patted him on the head and encouraged him gently, the dog seemed to reconcile himself to the situation, and followed me and F—— through the house, but keeping close at my heels, instead of hurrying inquisitively in advance, which was his usual and normal habit in all strange places. We first visited the subterranean apartments, the kitchen and other offices, and especially the cellars, in which last were two or three bottles of wine still left in a bin, covered with cobwebs, and evidently, by their appearance, undisturbed for many years. It was clear that the ghosts were not winebibbers. For the rest, we discovered nothing of interest. There was a gloomy little back yard, with very high walls. The stones of this yard were very damp; and what with the damp, and what with the dust and smoke-grime on the pavement, our feet left a slight impression where we passed. And now appeared the first strange phenomenon witnessed by myself in this strange abode. I saw, just before me, the print of a foot suddenly form itself, as it were. I stopped, caught hold of my servant, and pointed to it. In advance of that footprint as suddenly dropped another. We both saw it. I advanced quickly to the place; the footprint kept advancing before me; a small footprint,—the foot of a child; the impression was too faint thoroughly to distinguish the shape, but it seemed to us both that it was the print of a naked foot. This phenomenon ceased when we arrived at the opposite wall, nor did it repeat itself when we returned. We remounted the stairs, and entered the rooms on the ground-floor,—a dining-parlor, a small back parlor, and a still smaller third room, that had probably been appropriated to a footman,—all still as death. We then visited the drawing-rooms, which seemed fresh and new. In the front room I seated myself in an arm-chair. F—— placed on the table the candlestick with which he had lighted us. I told him to shut the door. As he turned to do so, a chair opposite to me moved from the wall quickly and noiselessly, and dropped itself about a yard from my own chair, immediately fronting it.

"Why, this is better than the turning tables," said I, with a half-laugh; and as I laughed, my dog put back his head and howled.

F——, coming back, had not observed the movement of the chair. He employed himself now in stilling the dog. I continued to gaze on the chair, and fancied I saw on it a pale, blue, misty outline of a human figure; but an outline so indistinct that I could only distrust my own vision. The dog was now quiet.

"Put back the chair opposite to me," said I to F——, "put it back to the wall."

F—— obeyed. "Was that you, sir?" said he, turning abruptly.

"I,—what?"

"Why, something struck me. I felt it sharply on the shoulder, just here."

"No," said I; "but we have jugglers present; and though we may not discover their tricks, we shall catch *them* before they frighten us."

We did not stay long in the drawing-rooms; in fact, they felt so damp and so chilly that I was glad to get to the fire up stairs. We locked the doors of the drawing-rooms,—a precaution which, I should observe, we had taken with all the rooms we had searched below. The bedroom my servant had selected for me was the best on the floor; a large one, with two windows fronting the street. The four-posted bed, which took up no inconsiderable space, was opposite to the fire, which burned clear and bright; a door in the wall to the left, between the bed and the window, communicated with the room which my servant appropriated to himself. This last was a small room with a sofa-bed, and had no communication with the landing-place; no other door but that which conducted to the bedroom I was to occupy. On either side of my fireplace was a cupboard, without locks, flush with the wall, and covered with the same dull-brown paper. We examined these cupboards; only hooks to suspend female dresses,—nothing else. We sounded the walls; evidently solid,—the outer walls of the building. Having finished the survey of these apartments, warmed myself a few moments, and lighted my cigar, I then, still accompanied by F——, went forth to complete my reconnoitre. In the landing-place there was another door; it was closed firmly. "Sir," said my servant in surprise, "I unlocked this door with all the others when I first came; it cannot have got locked from the inside, for it is a——"

Before he had finished his sentence, the door, which neither of us then was touching, opened quietly of itself. We looked at each other a single instant. The same thought seized both; some human agency might be detected here. I rushed in first, my servant followed. A small, blank, dreary room without furniture, a few empty boxes and hampers in a corner, a small window, the shutters closed,—not even a fireplace,—no other door but that by which we had entered, no carpet on the floor, and the floor seemed very old, uneven, worm-eaten, mended here and there, as was shown by the whiter patches on the wood; but no living being, and no visible place in which a living being could have hidden. As we stood gazing round, the door by which we had entered closed as quietly as it had before opened; we were imprisoned.

For the first time I felt a creep of undefinable horror. Not so my servant. "Why, they don't think to trap us, sir; I could break that trumpery door with a kick of my foot."

"Try first if it will open to your hand," said I, shaking off the vague apprehension that had seized me, "while I open the shutters and see what is without."

I unbarred the shutters: the window looked on the little back yard I have before described; there was no ledge without, nothing but sheer descent. No man getting out of that window would have found any footing till he had fallen on the stones below.

F—— meanwhile was vainly attempting to open the door. He now turned round to me and asked my permission to use force. And I should here state, in justice to the servant, that, far from evincing any superstitious terror, his nerve, composure, and even gayety amidst circumstances so extraordinary, compelled my admiration, and made me congratulate myself on having secured a companion in every way fitted to the occasion. I willingly gave him the permission he required. But, though he was a remarkably strong man, his force was as idle as his milder efforts; the door did not even shake to his stoutest kick. Breathless and panting, he desisted. I then tried the door myself, equally in vain. As I ceased from the effort, again that creep of horror came over me; but this time it was more cold and stubborn. I felt as if some strange and ghastly exhalation were rising from the chinks of that rugged floor and filling the atmosphere with a venomous influence hostile to human life. The door now very slowly and quietly opened as of its own accord. We precipitated ourselves into the landing-place. We both saw a large, pale light—as large as the human figure, but shapeless and unsubstantial—move before us and ascend the stairs that led from the landing into the attics. I followed the light, and my servant followed me. It entered, to the right of the landing, a small garret, of which the door stood open. I entered in the same instant. The light then collapsed into a small globule, exceedingly brilliant and vivid; rested a moment on a bed in the corner, quivered, and vanished. We approached the bed and examined it,—a half-tester, such as is commonly found in attics devoted to servants. On the drawers that stood near it we perceived an old faded silk kerchief, with the needle still left in the rent half repaired. The kerchief was covered with dust; probably it had belonged to the old woman who had last died in that house, and this might have been her sleeping-room. I had sufficient curiosity to open the drawers; there were a few odds and ends of female dress, and two letters tied round with a narrow ribbon of faded yellow. I took the liberty to possess myself of the letters. We found nothing else in the room worth noticing, nor did the light reappear; but we distinctly heard, as we turned to go, a pattering footfall on the floor just before us. We went through the other attics (in all four), the footfall still preceding us. Nothing to be seen, nothing but the footfall heard. I had the letters in my hand; just as I was descending the stairs I distinctly felt my wrist seized, and a faint, soft effort made to draw the letters from my clasp. I only held them the more tightly, and the effort ceased.

We regained the bedchamber appropriated to myself, and I then remarked that my dog had not followed us when we had left it. He was thrusting himself close to the fire and trembling. I was impatient to examine the letters; and while I read them my servant opened a little box in which he had deposited the weapons I had ordered him to bring, took them out, placed them on a table close at my bed-head, and then occupied himself in soothing the dog, who, however, seemed to heed him very little.

The letters were short; they were dated,—the dates exactly thirty-five years ago. They were evidently from a lover to his mistress, or a husband to some young wife. Not only the terms of expression, but a distinct reference to a former voyage indicated the writer to have been a seafarer. The spelling and handwriting were those of a man imperfectly educated; but still the language itself was forcible. In the expressions of endearment there was a kind of rough, wild love; but here and there were dark unintelligible hints at some secret not of love,—some secret that seemed of crime. "We ought to love each other," was one of the sentences I remember, "for how every one else would execrate us if all was known." Again: "Don't let any one be in the same room with you at night,—you talk in your sleep." And again:

"What's done can't be undone: and I tell you there's nothing against us, unless the dead could come to life." Here was interlined, in a better handwriting (a female's), "They do!" At the end of the letter latest in date the same female hand had written these words: "Lost at sea the 4th of June, the same day as—"

I put down the letters, and began to muse over their contents.

Fearing, however, that the train of thought into which I fell might unsteady my nerves, I fully determined to keep my mind in a fit state to cope with whatever of marvellous the advancing night might bring forth. I roused myself, laid the letters on the table, stirred up the fire, which was still bright and cheering, and opened my volume of Macaulay. I read quietly enough, till about half past eleven. I then threw myself dressed upon the bed, and told my servant he might retire to his own room, but must keep himself awake. I bade him leave open the doors between the two rooms. Thus, alone, I kept two candles burning on the table by my bed-head. I placed my watch beside the weapons, and calmly resumed my Macaulay. Opposite to me the fire burned clear; and on the hearth-rug, seemingly asleep, lay the dog. In about twenty minutes I felt an exceedingly cold air pass by my cheek, like a sudden draught. I fancied the door to my right, communicating with the landing-place, must have got open; but no, it was closed. I then turned my glance to the left, and saw the flame of the candles violently swayed as by a wind. At the same moment the watch beside the revolver softly slid from the table,—softly, softly,—no visible hand,—it was gone. I sprang up, seizing the revolver with the one hand, the dagger with the other: I was not willing that my weapons should share the fate of the watch. Thus armed, I looked round the floor: no sign of the watch. Three slow, loud, distinct knocks were now heard at the bed-head; my servant called out, "Is that you, sir?"

"No; be on your guard."

The dog now roused himself and sat on his haunches, his ears moving quickly backward and forward. He kept his eye fixed on me with a look so strange that he concentred all my attention on himself. Slowly he rose, all his hair bristling, and stood perfectly rigid, and with the same wild stare. I had no time, however, to examine the dog. Presently my servant emerged from his room; and if I ever saw horror in the human face, it was then. I should not have recognized him had we met in the streets, so altered was every lineament. He passed by me quickly, saying in a whisper that seemed scarcely to come from his lips, "Run! run! it is after me!" He gained the door to the landing, pulled it open, and rushed forth. I followed him into the landing involuntarily, calling him to stop; but, without heeding me, he bounded down the stairs, clinging to the balusters and taking several steps at a time. I heard, where I stood, the street door open, heard it again clap to. I was left alone in the haunted house.

It was but for a moment that I remained undecided whether or not to follow my servant; pride and curiosity alike forbade so dastardly a flight. I re-entered my room, closing the door after me, and proceeded cautiously into the interior chamber. I encountered nothing to justify my servant's terror. I again carefully examined the walls, to see if there were any concealed door. I could find no trace of one,—not even a seam in the dull-brown paper with which the room was hung. How then had the THING, whatever it was, which had so scared him, obtained ingress, except through my own chamber?

I returned to my room, shut and locked the door that opened upon the interior one, and stood on the hearth, expectant and prepared. I now perceived that the dog had slunk into an angle of the wall, and was pressing close against it, as if literally striving to force his way into it. I approached the animal and spoke to it; the poor brute was evidently beside itself with terror. It showed all its teeth, the slaver dropping from its jaws, and would certainly have bitten me if I had touched it. It did not seem to recognize me. Whoever has seen at the Zoölogical Gardens a rabbit fascinated by a serpent, cowering in a corner, may form some idea of the anguish which the dog exhibited. Finding all efforts to soothe the animal in vain, and fearing that his bite might be as venomous in that state as if in the madness of hydrophobia, I left him alone, placed my weapons on the table beside the fire, seated myself, and recommenced my Macaulay.

Perhaps, in order not to appear seeking credit for a courage, or rather a coolness, which the reader may conceive I exaggerate, I may be pardoned if I pause to indulge in one or two egotistical remarks.

As I hold presence of mind, or what is called courage, to be precisely proportioned to familiarity with the circumstances that lead to it, so I should say that I had been long sufficiently familiar with all experiments that appertain to the marvellous. I had witnessed many very extraordinary phenomena in various parts of the world,—phenomena that would be either totally disbelieved if I stated them, or ascribed to supernatural agencies. Now, my theory is, that the supernatural is the impossible, and that what is called supernatural is only a something in the laws of nature of which we have been hitherto ignorant. Therefore, if a ghost rise before me, I have not the right to say, "So, then, the supernatural is possible," but rather, "So, then, the apparition of a ghost is, contrary to received opinion, within the laws of nature, namely, not supernatural."

Now, in all that I had hitherto witnessed, and indeed in all the wonders which the amateurs of mystery in our age record as facts, a material living agency is always required. On the Continent you will find still magicians who assert that they can raise spirits. Assume for the moment that they assert truly, still the living material form of the magician is present; and he is the material agency by which, from some constitutional peculiarities, certain strange phenomena are represented to your natural senses.

Accept, again, as truthful the tales of spirit manifestation in America,— musical or other sounds, writings on paper, produced by no discernible hand, articles of furniture moved without apparent human agency, or the actual sight and touch of hands, to which no bodies seem to belong,—still there must be found the medium, or living being, with constitutional peculiarities capable of obtaining these signs. In fine, in all such marvels, supposing even that there is no imposture, there must be a human being like ourselves, by whom or through whom the effects presented to human beings are produced. It is so with the now familiar phenomena of mesmerism or electro-biology; the mind of the person operated on is affected through a material living agent. Nor, supposing it true that a mesmerized patient can respond to the will or passes of a mesmerizer a hundred miles distant, is the response less occasioned by a material being. It may be through a material fluid, call it Electric, call it Odic, call it what you will, which has the power of traversing space and passing obstacles, that the material effect is communicated from one to the other. Hence, all that I had hitherto witnessed, or expected to witness, in this strange house, I believed to be occasioned through some agency or medium as mortal as myself; and this idea necessarily prevented the awe with which those who regard as supernatural things that are not within the ordinary operations of nature might have been impressed by the adventures of that memorable night.

As, then, it was my conjecture that all that was presented, or would be presented, to my senses, must originate in some human being gifted by constitution with the power so to present them, and having some motive so to do, I felt an interest in my theory which, in its way, was rather philosophical than superstitious. And I can sincerely say that I was in as tranquil a temper for observation as any practical experimentalist could be in awaiting the effects of some rare, though perhaps perilous, chemical combination. Of course, the more I kept my mind detached from fancy, the more the temper fitted for observation would be obtained; and I therefore riveted eye and thought on the strong daylight sense in the page of my Macaulay.

I now became aware that something interposed between the page and the light: the page was overshadowed. I looked up and I saw what I shall find it very difficult, perhaps impossible, to describe.

It was a darkness shaping itself out of the air in very undefined outline. I cannot say it was of a human form, and yet it had more of a resemblance to a human form, or rather shadow, than anything else. As it stood, wholly apart and distinct from the air and the light around it, its dimensions seemed gigantic; the summit nearly touched the ceiling. While I gazed, a feeling of intense cold seized me. An iceberg before me could not more have chilled me; nor could the cold of an iceberg have been more purely physical. I feel convinced that it was not the cold caused by fear. As I continued to gaze, I thought—but this I cannot say with precision—that I distinguished two eyes looking down on me from the height. One moment I seemed to distinguish them clearly, the next they seemed gone; but two rays of a pale blue light frequently shot through the darkness, as from the height on which I half believed, half doubted, that I had encountered the eyes.

I strove to speak; my voice utterly failed me. I could only think to myself, "Is this fear? it is *not* fear!" I strove to rise, in vain; I felt as if weighed down by an irresistible force. Indeed, my impression was that of an immense and overwhelming power opposed to my volition; that sense of utter inadequacy to cope with a force beyond men's, which one may feel *physically* in a storm at sea, in a conflagration, or when confronting some terrible wild beast, or rather, perhaps, the shark of the ocean, I felt *morally*. Opposed to my will was another will, as far superior to its strength as storm, fire, and shark are superior in material force to the force of men.

And now, as this impression grew on me, now came, at last, horror,— horror to a degree that no words can convey. Still I retained pride, if not courage; and in my own mind I said, "This is horror, but it is not fear; unless I fear, I cannot be harmed; my reason rejects this thing; it is an illusion, I do not fear." With a violent effort I succeeded at last in stretching out my hand towards the weapon on the table; as I did so, on the arm and shoulder I received a strange shock, and my arm fell to my side powerless. And now, to add to my horror, the light began slowly to wane from the candles; they were not, as it were, extinguished, but their flame seemed very gradually withdrawn; it was the same with the fire, the light was extracted from the fuel; in a few minutes the room was in utter darkness. The dread that came over me to be thus in the dark with that dark thing, whose power was so intensely felt, brought a reaction of nerve. In fact, terror had reached that climax, that either my senses must have deserted me, or I must have burst through the spell. I did burst through it. I found voice, though the voice was a shriek. I remember that I broke forth with words like these, "I do not fear, my soul does not fear"; and at the same time I found strength to rise. Still in that profound gloom I rushed to one of the windows, tore aside the curtain, flung open the shutters; my first thought was, LIGHT.

And when I saw the moon, high, clear, and calm, I felt a joy that almost compensated for the previous terror. There was the moon, there was also the light from the gas-lamps in the deserted, slumberous street. I turned to look back into the room; the moon penetrated its shadow very palely and partially, but still there was light. The dark thing, whatever it might be, was gone; except that I could yet see a dim shadow, which seemed the shadow of that shade, against the opposite wall.

My eye now rested on the table, and from under the table (which was without cloth or cover, an old mahogany round table) rose a hand, visible as far as the wrist. It was a hand, seemingly, as much of flesh and blood as my own, but the hand of an aged person, lean, wrinkled, small too, a woman's hand. That hand very softly closed on the two letters that lay on the table; hand and letters both vanished. Then came the same three loud measured knocks I had heard at the bed-head before this extraordinary drama had commenced.

As these sounds slowly ceased, I felt the whole room vibrate sensibly; and at the far end rose, as from the floor, sparks or globules like bubbles of light, many-colored,—green, yellow, fire-red, azure,—up and down, to and fro, hither, thither, as tiny will-o'-the-wisps the sparks moved, slow or swift, each at its own caprice. A chair (as in the drawing-room below) was now advanced from the wall without apparent agency, and placed at the opposite side of the table. Suddenly, as forth from the chair, grew a shape, a woman's shape. It was distinct as a shape of life, ghastly as a shape of death. The face was that of youth, with a strange, mournful beauty; the throat and shoulders were bare, the rest of the form in a loose robe of cloudy white. It began sleeking its long yellow hair, which fell over its shoulders; its eyes were not turned toward me, but to the door; it seemed listening, watching, waiting. The shadow of the shade in the background grew darker; and again I thought I beheld the eyes gleaming out from the summit of the shadow, eyes fixed upon that shape.

As if from the door, though it did not open, grew out another shape, equally distinct, equally ghastly,—a man's shape, a young man's. It was in the dress of the last century, or rather in a likeness of such dress; for both the male shape and the female, though defined, were evidently unsubstantial, impalpable,—simulacra, phantasms; and there was something incongruous, grotesque, yet fearful, in the contrast between the elaborate finery, the courtly precision of that old-fashioned garb, with its ruffles and lace and buckles, and the corpse-like aspect and ghost-like stillness of the flitting wearer. Just as the male shape approached the female, the dark shadow darted from the wall, all three for a moment wrapped in darkness. When the pale light returned, the two phantoms were as if in the grasp of the shadow that towered between them, and there was a blood-stain on the breast of the female; and the phantom male was leaning on its phantom sword, and blood seemed trickling fast from the ruffles, from the lace; and the darkness of the intermediate shadow swallowed them up, they were gone. And again the bubbles of light shot, and sailed, and undulated, growing thicker and thicker and more wildly confused in their movements.

The closet door to the right of the fireplace now opened, and from the aperture came the form of a woman, aged. In her hand she held letters,— the very letters over which I had seen *the* hand close; and behind her I heard a footstep. She turned round as if to listen, and then she opened the letters and seemed to read: and over her shoulder I saw a livid face, the face as of a man long drowned,—bloated, bleached, seaweed tangled in its dripping hair; and at her feet lay a form as of a corpse, and beside the corpse cowered a child, a miserable, squalid child, with famine in its cheeks and fear in its eyes. And as I looked in the old woman's face, the wrinkles and lines vanished, and it became a face of youth,—hard-eyed, stony, but still youth; and the shadow darted forth and darkened over these phantoms, as it had darkened over the last.

Nothing now was left but the shadow, and on that my eyes were intently fixed, till again eyes grew out of the shadow,—malignant, serpent eyes. And the bubbles of light again rose and fell, and in their disordered, irregular, turbulent maze mingled with the wan moonlight. And now from these globules themselves, as from the shell of an egg, monstrous things burst out; the air grew filled with them; larvæ so bloodless and so hideous that I can in no way describe them, except to remind the reader of the swarming life which the solar microscope brings before his eyes in a drop of water,— things transparent, supple, agile, chasing each other, devouring each other,—forms like naught ever beheld by the naked eye. As the shapes were without symmetry, so their movements were without order. In their very vagrancies there was no sport; they came round me and round, thicker and faster and swifter, swarming over my head, crawling over my right arm, which was outstretched in involuntary command against all evil beings. Sometimes I felt myself touched, but not by them; invisible hands touched me. Once I felt the clutch as of cold, soft fingers at my throat. I was still equally conscious that if I gave way to fear I should be in bodily peril, and I concentred all my faculties in the single focus of resisting, stubborn will. And I turned my sight from the shadow, above all from those strange serpent eyes,—eyes that had now become distinctly visible. For there, though in naught else around me, I was aware that there was a will, and a will of intense, creative, working evil, which might crush down my own.

The pale atmosphere in the room began now to redden as if in the air of some near conflagration. The larvæ grew lurid as things that live in fire. Again the room vibrated; again were heard the three measured knocks; and again all things were swallowed up in the darkness of the dark shadow, as if out of that darkness all had come, into that darkness all returned.

As the gloom receded, the shadow was wholly gone. Slowly as it had been withdrawn, the flame grew again into the candles on the table, again into the fuel in the grate. The whole room came once more calmly, healthfully into sight.

The two doors were still closed, the door communicating with the servant's room still locked. In the corner of the wall, into which he had convulsively niched himself, lay the dog. I called to him,—no movement; I approached,—the animal was dead; his eyes protruded, his tongue out of his mouth, the froth gathered round his jaws. I took him in my arms; I brought him to the fire; I felt acute grief for the loss of my poor favorite, acute self-reproach; I accused myself of his death; I imagined he had died of fright. But what was my surprise on finding that his neck was actually broken,—actually twisted out of the vertebræ. Had this been done in the dark? Must it not have been done by a hand human as mine? Must there not have been a human agency all the while in that room? Good cause to suspect it. I cannot tell. I cannot do more than state the fact fairly; the reader may draw his own inference.

Another surprising circumstance,—my watch was restored to the table from which it had been so mysteriously withdrawn; but it had stopped at the very moment it was so withdrawn; nor, despite all the skill of the watchmaker, has it ever gone since: that is, it will go in a strange, erratic way for a few hours, and then comes to a dead stop; it is worthless.

Nothing more chanced for the rest of the night; nor, indeed, had I long to wait before the dawn broke. Not till it was broad daylight did I quit the haunted house. Before I did so, I revisited the little blind room in which my servant and I had been for a time imprisoned. I had a strong impression, for which I could not account, that from that room had originated the mechanism of the phenomena, if I may use the term, which had been experienced in my chamber; and though I entered it now in the clear day, with the sun peering through the filmy window, I still felt, as I stood on its floor, the creep of the horror which I had first experienced there the night before, and which had been so aggravated by what had passed in my own chamber. I could not, indeed, bear to stay more than half a minute within those walls. I descended the stairs, and again I heard the footfall before me; and when I opened the street door I thought I could distinguish a very low laugh. I gained my own home, expecting to find my runaway servant there. But he had not presented himself; nor did I hear more of him for three days, when I received a letter from him, dated from Liverpool, to this effect:—

"HONORED SIR,—I humbly entreat your pardon, though I can scarcely hope that you will think I deserve it, unless—which Heaven forbid!—you saw what I did. I feel that it will be years before I can recover myself; and as to being fit for service, it is out of the question. I am therefore going to my brother-in-law at Melbourne. The ship sails to-morrow. Perhaps the long voyage may set me up. I do nothing now but start and tremble, and fancy it is behind me. I humbly beg you, honored sir, to order my clothes, and whatever wages are due to me, to be sent to my mother's at Walworth: John knows her address."

The letter ended with additional apologies, somewhat incoherent, and explanatory details as to effects that had been under the writer's charge.

This flight may perhaps warrant a suspicion that the man wished to go to Australia, and had been somehow or other fraudulently mixed up with the events of the night. I say nothing in refutation of that conjecture; rather, I suggest it as one that would seem to many persons the most probable solution of improbable occurrences. My own theory remained unshaken. I returned in the evening to the house, to bring away in a hack cab the things I had left there, with my poor dog's body. In this task I was not disturbed, nor did any incident worth note befall me, except that still, on ascending and descending the stairs, I heard the same footfall in advance. On leaving the house, I went to Mr. J——'s. He was at home. I returned him the keys, told him that my curiosity was sufficiently gratified, and was about to relate quickly what had passed, when he stopped me and said, though with much politeness, that he had no longer any interest in a mystery which none had ever solved.

I determined at least to tell him of the two letters I had read, as well as of the extraordinary manner in which they had disappeared; and I then inquired if he thought they had been addressed to the woman who had died in the house, and if there were anything in her early history which could possibly confirm the dark suspicions to which the letters gave rise. Mr. J—— seemed startled, and, after musing a few moments, answered: "I know but little of the woman's earlier history, except, as I before told you, that her family were known to mine. But you revive some vague reminiscences to her prejudice. I will make inquiries, and inform you of their result. Still, even if we could admit the popular superstition that a person who had been either the perpetrator or the victim of dark crimes in life could revisit, as a restless spirit, the scene in which those crimes had been committed, I should observe that the house was infested by strange sights and sounds before the old woman died. You smile; what would you say?"

"I would say this: that I am convinced, if we could get to the bottom of these mysteries, we should find a living, human agency."

"What! you believe it is all an imposture? For what object?"

"Not an imposture, in the ordinary sense of the word. If suddenly I were to sink into a deep sleep, from which you could not awake me, but in that deep sleep could answer questions with an accuracy which I could not pretend to when awake,—tell you what money you had in your pocket, nay, describe your very thoughts,—it is not necessarily an imposture, any more than it is necessarily supernatural. I should be, unconsciously to myself, under a mesmeric influence, conveyed to me from a distance by a human being who had acquired power over me by previous *rapport*."

"Granting mesmerism, so far carried, to be a fact, you are right. And you would infer from this that a mesmerizer might produce the extraordinary effects you and others have witnessed over inanimate objects,—fill the air with sights and sounds?"

"Or impress our senses with the belief in them, we never having been *en rapport* with the person acting on us? No. What is commonly called mesmerism could not do this; but there may be a power akin to mesmerism, and superior to it,—the power that in the old days was called Magic. That such a power may extend to all inanimate objects of matter, I do not say; but if so, it would not be against nature, only a rare power in nature, which might be given to constitutions with certain peculiarities, and cultivated by practice to an extraordinary degree. That such a power might extend over the dead,—that is, over certain thoughts and memories that the dead may still retain,—and compel, not that which ought properly to be called the soul, and which is far beyond human reach, but rather a phantom of what has been most earth-stained on earth, to make itself apparent to our senses,—is a very ancient though obsolete theory, upon which I will hazard no opinion. But I do not conceive the power would be supernatural. Let me illustrate what I mean, from an experiment which Paracelsus describes as not difficult, and which the author of the 'Curiosities of Literature' cites as credible: A flower perishes; you burn it. Whatever were the elements of that flower while it lived are gone, dispersed, you know not whither; you can never discover nor re-collect them. But you can, by chemistry, out of the burnt dust of that flower, raise a spectrum of the flower, just as it seemed in life. It may be the same with a human being. The soul has as much escaped you as the essence or elements of the flower. Still you may make a spectrum of it. And this phantom, though in the popular superstition it is held to be the soul of the departed, must not be confounded with the true soul; it is but the eidolon of the dead form. Hence, like the best-attested stories of ghosts or spirits, the thing that most strikes us is the absence of what we hold to be soul,—that is, of superior, emancipated intelligence. They come for little or no object; they seldom speak, if they do come; they utter no ideas above those of an ordinary person on earth. These American spiritseers have published volumes of communications in prose and verse, which they assert to be given in the names of the most illustrious dead,—Shakespeare, Bacon, Heaven knows whom. Those communications, taking the best, are certainly of not a whit higher order than would be communications from living persons of fair talent and education; they are wondrously inferior to what Bacon, Shakespeare, and Plato said and wrote when on earth. Nor, what is more notable, do they ever contain an idea that was not on the earth before. Wonderful, therefore, as such phenomena may be (granting them to be truthful), I see much that philosophy may question, nothing that it is incumbent on philosophy to deny, namely, nothing supernatural. They are but ideas conveyed somehow or other (we have not yet discovered the means) from one mortal brain to another. Whether in so doing tables walk of their own accord, or fiend-like shapes appear in a magic circle, or bodiless hands rise and remove material objects, or a thing of darkness, such as presented itself to me, freeze our blood,—still am I persuaded that these are but agencies conveyed, as by electric wires, to my own brain from the brain of another. In some constitutions there is a natural chemistry, and those may produce chemic wonders; in others a natural fluid, call it electricity, and these produce electric wonders. But they differ in this from normal science: they are alike objectless, purposeless, puerile, frivolous. They lead on to no grand results, and therefore the world does not heed, and true sages have not cultivated them. But sure I am, that of all I saw or heard, a man, human as myself, was the remote originator; and, I believe, unconsciously to himself as to the exact effects produced, for this reason: no two persons, you say, have ever told you that they experienced exactly the same thing; well, observe, no two persons ever experience exactly the same dream. If this were an ordinary imposture, the machinery would be arranged for results that would but little vary; if it were a supernatural agency permitted by the Almighty, it would surely be for some definite end. These phenomena belong to neither class. My persuasion is, that they originate in some brain now far distant; that that brain had no distinct volition in anything that occurred; that what does occur reflects but its devious, motley, ever-shifting, half-formed thoughts; in short, that it has been but the dreams of such a brain put into action and invested with a semi-substance. That this brain is of immense power, that it can set matter into movement, that it is malignant and destructive, I believe. Some material force must have killed my dog; it might, for aught I know, have sufficed to kill myself, had I been as subjugated by terror as the dog,—had my intellect or my spirit given me no countervailing resistance in my will."

"It killed your dog! that is fearful! Indeed, it is strange that no animal can be induced to stay in that house; not even a cat. Rats and mice are never found in it."

"The instincts of the brute creation detect influences deadly to their existence. Man's reason has a sense less subtle, because it has a resisting power more supreme. But enough; do you comprehend my theory?"

"Yes, though imperfectly; and I accept any crotchet (pardon the word), however odd, rather than embrace at once the notion of ghosts and hobgoblins we imbibed in our nurseries. Still, to my unfortunate house the evil is the same. What on earth can I do with the house?"

"I will tell you what I would do. I am convinced from my own internal feelings that the small unfurnished room, at right angles to the door of the bedroom which I occupied, forms a starting-point or receptacle for the influences which haunt the house; and I strongly advise you to have the walls opened, the floor removed, nay, the whole room pulled down. I observe that it is detached from the body of the house, built over the small back yard, and could be removed without injury to the rest of the building."

"And you think if I did that—"

"You would cut off the telegraph-wires. Try it. I am so persuaded that I am right, that I will pay half the expense, if you will allow me to direct the operations."

"Nay, I am well able to afford the cost; for the rest, allow me to write to you."

About ten days afterwards I received a letter from Mr. J——, telling me that he had visited the house since I had seen him; that he had found the two letters I had described replaced in the drawer from which I had taken them; that he had read them with misgivings like my own; that he had instituted a cautious inquiry about the woman to whom I rightly conjectured they had been written. It seemed that thirty-six years ago (a year before the date of the letters) she had married, against the wish of her relatives, an American of very suspicious character; in fact, he was generally believed to have been a pirate. She herself was the daughter of very respectable tradespeople, and had served in the capacity of nursery governess before her marriage. She had a brother, a widower, who was considered wealthy, and who had one child about six years old. A month after the marriage, the body of this brother was found in the Thames, near London Bridge; there seemed some marks of violence about his throat, but they were not deemed sufficient to warrant the inquest in any other verdict than that of "found drowned."

The American and his wife took charge of the little boy, the deceased brother having by his will left his sister the guardian of his only child, and in event of the child's death the sister inherited. The child died about six months afterward; it was supposed to have been neglected and ill-treated.

The neighbors deposed to have heard it shriek at night. The surgeon who had examined it after death said that it was emaciated as if from want of nourishment, and the body was covered with livid bruises. It seemed that one winter night the child had sought to escape; had crept out into the back yard, tried to scale the wall, fallen back exhausted, and had been found at morning on the stones in a dying state. But though there was some evidence of cruelty, there was none of murder; and the aunt and her husband had sought to palliate cruelty by alleging the exceeding stubbornness and perversity of the child, who was declared to be half-witted. Be that as it may, at the orphan's death the aunt inherited her brother's fortune. Before the first wedded year was out, the American quitted England abruptly, and never returned to it. He obtained a cruising vessel, which was lost in the Atlantic two years afterwards. The widow was left in affluence; but reverses of various kinds had befallen her; a bank broke, an investment failed, she went into a small business and became insolvent, then she entered into service, sinking lower and lower, from housekeeper down to maid-of-all-work, never long retaining a place, though nothing peculiar against her character was ever alleged. She was considered sober, honest, and peculiarly quiet in her ways; still nothing prospered with her. And so she had dropped into the workhouse, from which Mr. J—— had taken her, to be placed in charge of the very house which she had rented as mistress in the first year of her wedded life.

Mr. J—— added, that he had passed an hour alone in the unfurnished room which I had urged him to destroy, and that his impressions of dread while there were so great, though he had neither heard nor seen anything, that he was eager to have the walls bared and the floors removed, as I had suggested. He had engaged persons for the work, and would commence any day I would name.

The day was accordingly fixed. I repaired to the haunted house; we went into the blind, dreary room, took up the skirting, and then the floors. Under the rafters, covered with rubbish, was found a trap-door, quite large enough to admit a man. It was closely nailed down with clamps and rivets of iron. On removing these we descended into a room below, the existence of which had never been suspected. In this room there had been a window and a flue, but they had been bricked over, evidently for many years. By the help of candles we examined this place; it still retained some mouldering furniture,—three chairs, an oak settee, a table,—all of the fashion of about eighty years ago. There was a chest of drawers against the wall, in which we found, half rotted away, old-fashioned articles of a man's dress, such as might have been worn eighty or a hundred years ago, by a gentleman of some rank; costly steel buckles and buttons, like those yet worn in court-dresses, a handsome court-sword; in a waistcoat which had once been rich with gold-lace, but which was now blackened and foul with damp, we found five guineas, a few silver coins, and an ivory ticket, probably for some place of entertainment long since passed away. But our main discovery was in a kind of iron safe fixed to the wall, the lock of which it cost us much trouble to get picked.

In this safe were three shelves and two small drawers. Ranged on the shelves were several small bottles of crystal, hermetically stopped. They contained colorless volatile essences, of what nature I shall say no more than that they were not poisons; phosphor and ammonia entered into some of them. There were also some very curious glass tubes, and a small pointed rod of iron, with a large lump of rock-crystal, and another of amber, also a loadstone of great power.

In one of the drawers we found a miniature portrait set in gold, and retaining the freshness of its colors most remarkably, considering the length of time it had probably been there. The portrait was that of a man who might be somewhat advanced in middle life, perhaps forty-seven or forty-eight.

It was a most peculiar face, a most impressive face. If you could fancy some mighty serpent transformed into man, preserving in the human lineaments the old serpent type, you would have a better idea of that countenance than long descriptions can convey; the width and flatness of frontal, the tapering elegance of contour, disguising the strength of the deadly jaw; the long, large, terrible eye, glittering and green as the emerald, and withal a certain ruthless calm, as if from the consciousness of an immense power. The strange thing was this: the instant I saw the miniature I recognized a startling likeness to one of the rarest portraits in the world; the portrait of a man of rank only below that of royalty, who in his own day had made a considerable noise. History says little or nothing of him; but search the correspondence of his contemporaries, and you find reference to his wild daring, his bold profligacy, his restless spirit, his taste for the occult sciences. While still in the meridian of life he died and was buried, so say the chronicles, in a foreign land. He died in time to escape the grasp of the law; for he was accused of crimes which would have given him to the headsman. After his death, the portraits of him, which had been numerous, for he had been a munificent encourager of art, were bought up and destroyed, it was supposed by his heirs, who might have been glad could they have razed his very name from their splendid line. He had enjoyed vast wealth; a large portion of this was believed to have been embezzled by a favorite astrologer or soothsayer; at all events, it had unaccountably vanished at the time of his death. One portrait alone of him was supposed to have escaped the general destruction; I had seen it in the house of a collector some months before. It had made on me a wonderful impression, as it does on all who behold it; a face never to be forgotten; and there was that face in the miniature that lay within my hand. True, that in the miniature the man was a few years older than in the portrait I had seen, or than the original was even at the time of his death. But a few years!—why, between the date in which flourished that direful noble, and the date in which the miniature was evidently painted, there was an interval of more than two centuries. While I was thus gazing, silent and wondering, Mr. J—— said,—

"But is it possible? I have known this man."

"How? where?" cried I.

"In India. He was high in the confidence of the Rajah of——, and wellnigh drew him into a revolt which would have lost the Rajah his dominions. The man was a Frenchman, his name De V——; clever, bold, lawless. We insisted on his dismissal and banishment; it must be the same man, no two faces like his, yet this miniature seems nearly a hundred years old."

Mechanically I turned round the miniature to examine the back of it, and on the back was engraved a pentacle; in the middle of the pentacle a ladder, and the third step of the ladder was formed by the date 1765. Examining still more minutely, I detected a spring; this, on being pressed, opened the back of the miniature as a lid. Within-side the lid were engraved, "Mariana, to thee. Be faithful in life and in death to——." Here follows a name that I will not mention, but it was not unfamiliar to me. I had heard it spoken of by old men in my childhood as the name borne by a dazzling charlatan, who had made a great sensation in London for a year or so, and had fled the country on the charge of a double murder within his own house,—that of his mistress and his rival. I said nothing of this to Mr. J——, to whom reluctantly I resigned the miniature.

We had found no difficulty in opening the first drawer within the iron safe; we found great difficulty in opening the second: it was not locked, but it resisted all efforts, till we inserted in the chinks the edge of a chisel. When we had thus drawn it forth, we found a very singular apparatus, in the nicest order. Upon a small, thin book, or rather tablet, was placed a saucer of crystal; this saucer was filled with a clear liquid; on that liquid floated a kind of compass, with a needle shifting rapidly round; but instead of the usual points of a compass, were seven strange characters, not very unlike those used by astrologers to denote the planets. A very peculiar, but not strong nor displeasing odor came from this drawer, which was lined with a wood that we afterward discovered to be hazel. Whatever the cause of this odor, it produced a material effect on the nerves. We all felt it, even the two workmen who were in the room; a creeping, tingling sensation, from the tips of the fingers to the roots of the hair. Impatient to examine the tablet, I removed the saucer. As I did so, the needle of the compass went round and round with exceeding swiftness, and I felt a shock that ran through my whole frame, so that I dropped the saucer on the floor. The liquid was spilt, the saucer was broken, the compass rolled to the end of the room, and at that instant the walls shook to and fro as if a giant had swayed and rocked them.

The two workmen were so frightened that they ran up the ladder by which we had descended from the trap-door; but, seeing that nothing more happened, they were easily induced to return.

Meanwhile, I had opened the tablet; it was bound in plain red leather, with a silver clasp; it contained but one sheet of thick vellum, and on that sheet were inscribed, within a double pentacle, words in old monkish Latin, which are literally to be translated thus: "On all that it can reach within these walls, sentient or inanimate, living or dead, as moves the needle, so works my will! Accursed be the house, and restless the dwellers therein."

We found no more. Mr. J—— burnt the tablet and its anathema. He razed to the foundation the part of the building containing the secret room, with the chamber over it. He had then the courage to inhabit the house himself for a month, and a quieter, better conditioned house could not be found in all London. Subsequently he let it to advantage, and his tenant has made no complaints.

But my story is not yet done. A few days after Mr. J—— had removed into the house, I paid him a visit. We were standing by the open window and conversing. A van containing some articles of furniture which he was moving from his former house was at the door. I had just urged on him my theory, that all those phenomena regarded as supermundane had emanated from a human brain; adducing the charm, or rather curse, we had found and destroyed, in support of my theory. Mr. J—— was observing in reply, "that even if mesmerism, or whatever analogous power it might be called, could really thus work in the absence of the operator, and produce effects so extraordinary, still could those effects continue when the operator himself was dead? and if the spell had been wrought, and, indeed, the room walled up, more than seventy years ago, the probability was, that the operator had long since departed this life,"—Mr. J——, I say, was thus answering, when I caught hold of his arm and pointed to the street below.

A well-dressed man had crossed from the opposite side, and was accosting the carrier in charge of the van. His face, as he stood, was exactly fronting our window. It was the face of the miniature we had discovered; it was the face of the portrait of the noble three centuries ago.

"Good heavens!" cried Mr. J——, "that is the face of De V——, and scarcely a day older than when I saw it in the Rajah's court in my youth!"

Seized by the same thought, we both hastened down stairs; I was first in the street, but the man had already gone. I caught sight of him, however, not many yards in advance, and in another moment I was by his side.

I had resolved to speak to him; but when I looked into his face, I felt as if it were impossible to do so. That eye—the eye of the serpent—fixed and held me spellbound. And withal, about the man's whole person there was a dignity, an air of pride and station and superiority, that would have made any one, habituated to the usages of the world, hesitate long before venturing upon a liberty or impertinence. And what could I say? What was it I could ask? Thus ashamed of my first impulse, I fell a few paces back, still, however, following the stranger, undecided what else to do. Meanwhile, he turned the corner of the street; a plain carriage was in waiting with a servant out of livery, dressed like a *valet de place*, at the carriage door. In another moment he had stepped into the carriage, and it drove off. I returned to the house. Mr. J—— was still at the street door. He had asked the carrier what the stranger had said to him.

"Merely asked whom that house now belonged to."

The same evening I happened to go with a friend to a place in town called the Cosmopolitan Club, a place open to men of all countries, all opinions, all degrees. One orders one's coffee, smokes one's cigar. One is always sure to meet agreeable, sometimes remarkable persons.

I had not been two minutes in the room before I beheld at table, conversing with an acquaintance of mine, whom I will designate by the initial G——, the man, the original of the miniature. He was now without his hat, and the likeness was yet more startling, only I observed that while he was conversing, there was less severity in the countenance; there was even a smile, though a very quiet and very cold one. The dignity of mien I had acknowledged in the street was also more striking; a dignity akin to that which invests some prince of the East, conveying the idea of supreme indifference and habitual, indisputable, indolent, but resistless power.

G—— soon after left the stranger, who then took up a scientific journal, which seemed to absorb his attention.

I drew G—— aside. "Who and what is that gentleman?"

"That? Oh, a very remarkable man indeed! I met him last year amidst the caves of Petra, the Scriptural Edom. He is the best Oriental scholar I know. We joined company, had an adventure with robbers, in which he showed a coolness that saved our lives; afterward he invited me to spend a day with him in a house he had bought at Damascus, a house buried amongst almond-blossoms and roses; the most beautiful thing! He had lived there for some years, quite as an Oriental, in grand style. I half suspect he is a renegade, immensely rich, very odd; by the by, a great mesmerizer. I have seen him with my own eyes produce an effect on inanimate things. If you take a letter from your pocket and throw it to the other end of the room, he will order it to come to his feet, and you will see the letter wriggle itself along the floor till it has obeyed his command. 'Pon my honor 'tis true; I have seen him affect even the weather; disperse or collect clouds, by means of a glass tube or wand. But he does not like talking of these matters to strangers. He has only just arrived in England; says he has not been here for a great many years; let me introduce him to you."

"Certainly! He is English, then? What is his name?"

"Oh! a very homely one,—Richards."

"And what is his birth,—his family?"

"How do I know? What does it signify? No doubt some *parvenu*; but rich, so infernally rich!"

G—— drew me up to the stranger, and the introduction was effected. The manners of Mr. Richards were not those of an adventurous traveller. Travellers are in general gifted with high animal spirits; they are talkative, eager, imperious. Mr. Richards was calm and subdued in tone, with manners which were made distant by the loftiness of punctilious courtesy, the manners of a former age. I observed that the English he spoke was not exactly of our day. I should even have said that the accent was slightly foreign. But then Mr. Richards remarked that he had been little in the habit for many years of speaking in his native tongue. The conversation fell upon the changes in the aspect of London since he had last visited our metropolis. G—— then glanced off to the moral changes,—literary, social, political,—the great men who were removed from the stage within the last twenty years; the new great men who were coming on. In all this Mr. Richards evinced no interest. He had evidently read none of our living authors, and seemed scarcely acquainted by name with our younger statesmen. Once, and only once, he laughed; it was when G—— asked him whether he had any thoughts of getting into Parliament. And the laugh was inward, sarcastic, sinister; a sneer raised into a laugh. After a few minutes, G—— left us to talk to some other acquaintances who had just lounged into the room, and I then said, quietly,—

"I have seen a miniature of you, Mr. Richards, in the house you once inhabited, and perhaps built,—if not wholly, at least in part,—in Oxford Street. You passed by that house this morning."

Not till I had finished did I raise my eyes to his, and then his fixed my gaze so steadfastly that I could not withdraw it,—those fascinating serpent-eyes. But involuntarily, and as if the words that translated my thought were dragged from me, I added in a low whisper, "I have been a student in the mysteries of life and nature; of those mysteries I have known the occult professors. I have the right to speak to you thus." And I uttered a certain password.

"Well, I concede the right. What would you ask?"

"To what extent human will in certain temperaments can extend?"

"To what extent can thought extend? Think, and before you draw breath you are in China!"

"True; but my thought has no power in China!"

"Give it expression, and it may have. You may write down a thought which, sooner or later, may alter the whole condition of China. What is a law but a thought? Therefore thought is infinite. Therefore thought has power; not in proportion to its value,—a bad thought may make a bad law as potent as a good thought can make a good one."

"Yes; what you say confirms my own theory. Through invisible currents one human brain may transmit its ideas to other human brains, with the same rapidity as a thought promulgated by visible means. And as thought is imperishable, as it leaves its stamp behind it in the natural world, even when the thinker has passed out of this world, so the thought of the living may have power to rouse up and revive the thoughts of the dead, such as those thoughts *were in life*, though the thought of the living cannot reach the thoughts which the dead *now* may entertain. Is it not so?"

"I decline to answer, if in my judgment thought has the limit you would fix to it. But proceed; you have a special question you wish to put."

"Intense malignity in an intense will, engendered in a peculiar temperament, and aided by natural means within the reach of science, may produce effects like those ascribed of old to evil magic. It might thus haunt the walls of a human habitation with spectral revivals of all guilty thoughts and guilty deeds once conceived and done within those walls; all, in short, with which the evil will claims *rapport* and affinity,—imperfect, incoherent, fragmentary snatches at the old dramas acted therein years ago. Thoughts thus crossing each other haphazard, as in the nightmare of a vision, growing up into phantom sights and sounds, and all serving to create horror; not because those sights and sounds are really visitations from a world without, but that they are ghastly, monstrous renewals of what have been in this world itself, set into malignant play by a malignant mortal. And it is through the material agency of that human brain that these things would acquire even a human power; would strike as with the shock of electricity, and might kill, if the thought of the person assailed did not rise superior to the dignity of the original assailer; might kill the most powerful animal, if unnerved by fear, but not injure the feeblest man, if, while his flesh crept, his mind stood out fearless. Thus when in old stories we read of a magician rent to pieces by the fiends he had invoked, or still more, in Eastern legends, that one magician succeeds by arts in destroying another, there may be so far truth, that a material being has clothed, from his own evil propensities, certain elements and fluids, usually quiescent or harmless, with awful shapes and terrific force; just as the lightning, that had lain hidden and innocent in the cloud, becomes by natural law suddenly risible, takes a distinct shape to the eye, and can strike destruction on the object to which it is attracted."

"You are not without glimpses of a mighty secret," said Mr. Richards, composedly. "According to your view, could a mortal obtain the power you speak of, he would necessarily be a malignant and evil being."

"If the power were exercised, as I have said, most malignant and most evil; though I believe in the ancient traditions, that he could not injure the good. His will could only injure those with whom it has established an affinity, or over whom it forces unresisted sway. I will now imagine an example that may be within the laws of nature, yet seem wild as the fables of a bewildered monk.

"You will remember that Albertus Magnus, after describing minutely the process by which spirits may be invoked and commanded, adds emphatically, that the process will instruct and avail only to the few; that *a man must be born a magician!* that is, born with a peculiar physical temperament, as a man is born a poet. Rarely are men in whose constitution lurks this occult power of the highest order of intellect; usually in the intellect there is some twist, perversity, or disease. But, on the other hand, they must possess, to an astonishing degree, the faculty to concentrate thought on a single object,—the energic faculty that we call WILL. Therefore, though their intellect be not sound, it is exceedingly forcible for the attainment of what it desires. I will imagine such a person, pre-eminently gifted with this constitution and its concomitant forces. I will place him in the loftier grades of society. I will suppose his desires emphatically those of the sensualist; he has, therefore, a strong love of life. He is an absolute egotist; his will is concentred in himself; he has fierce passions; he knows no enduring, no holy affections, but he can covet eagerly what for the moment he desires; he can hate implacably what opposes itself to his objects; he can commit fearful crimes, yet feel small remorse; he resorts rather to curses upon others, than to penitence for his misdeeds. Circumstances, to which his constitution guides him, lead him to a rare knowledge of the natural secrets which may serve his egotism. He is a close observer where his passions encourage observation; he is a minute calculator, not from love of truth, but where love of self sharpens his faculties; therefore he can be a man of science. I suppose such a being, having by experience learned the power of his arts over others, trying what may be the power of will over his own frame, and studying all that in natural philosophy may increase that power. He loves life, he dreads death; *he wills to live on.* He cannot restore himself to youth, he cannot entirely stay the progress of death, he cannot make himself immortal in the flesh and blood; but he may arrest, for a time so long as to appear incredible if I said it, that hardening of the parts which constitutes old age. A year may age him no more than an hour ages another. His intense will, scientifically trained into system, operates, in short, over the wear and tear of his own frame. He lives on. That he may not seem a portent and a miracle, he *dies*, from time to time, seemingly, to certain persons. Having schemed the transfer of a wealth that suffices to his wants, he disappears from one corner of the world, and contrives that his obsequies shall be celebrated. He reappears at another corner of the world, where he resides undetected, and does not visit the scenes of his former career till all who could remember his features are no more. He would be profoundly miserable if he had affections; he has none but for himself. No good man would accept his longevity; and to no man, good or bad, would he or could he communicate its true secret. Such a man might exist; such a man as I have described I see now before me,—Duke of——, in the court of——, dividing time between lust and brawl, alchemists and wizards; again, in the last century, charlatan and criminal, with name less noble, domiciled in the house at which you gazed to-day, and flying from the law you had outraged, none knew whither; traveller once more revisiting London, with the same earthly passions which filled your heart when races now no more walked through yonder streets; outlaw from the school of all the nobler and diviner mysteries. Execrable image of life in death and death in life, I warn you back from the cities and homes of healthful men! back to the ruins of departed empires! back to the deserts of nature unredeemed!"

There answered me a whisper so musical, so potently musical, that it seemed to enter into my whole being, and subdue me despite myself. Thus it said:—

"I have sought one like you for the last hundred years. Now I have found you, we part not till I know what I desire. The vision that sees through the past and cleaves through the veil of the future is in you at this hour,—never before, never to come again. The vision of no puling, fantastic girl, of no sick-bed somnambule, but of a strong man with a vigorous brain. Soar, and look forth!"

As he spoke, I felt as if I rose out of myself upon eagle wings. All the weight seemed gone from air, roofless the room, roofless the dome of space. I was not in the body,—where, I knew not; but aloft over time, over earth.

Again I heard the melodious whisper: "You say right. I have mastered great secrets by the power of will. True, by will and by science I can retard the process of years; but death comes not by age alone. Can I frustrate the accidents which bring death upon the young?"

"No; every accident is a providence. Before a providence, snaps every human will."

"Shall I die at last, ages and ages hence, by the slow, though inevitable, growth of time, or by the cause that I call accident?"

"By a cause you call accident."

"Is not the end still remote?" asked the whisper, with a slight tremor.

"Regarded as my life regards time, it is still remote."

"And shall I, before then, mix with the world of men as I did ere I learned these secrets; resume eager interest in their strife and their trouble; battle with ambition, and use the power of the sage to win the power that belongs to kings?"

"You will yet play a part on the earth that will fill earth with commotion and amaze. For wondrous designs have you, a wonder yourself, been permitted to live on through the centuries. All the secrets you have stored will then have their uses; all that now makes you a stranger amidst the generations will contribute then to make you their lord. As the trees and the straws are drawn into a whirlpool, as they spin round, are sucked to the deep, and again tossed aloft by the eddies, so shall races and thrones be drawn into your vortex. Awful destroyer! but in destroying, made, against your own will, a constructor."

"And that date, too, is far off?"

"Far off; when it comes, think your end in this world is at hand!"

"How and what is the end? Look east, west, south, and north."

"In the north, where you never yet trod, toward the point whence your instincts have warned you, there a spectre will seize you. 'Tis Death! I see a ship! it is haunted; 'tis chased! it sails on. Baffled navies sail after that ship. It enters the region of ice. It passes a sky red with meteors. Two moons stand on high, over ice-reefs. I see the ship locked between white defiles; they are ice-rocks. I see the dead strew the decks, stark and livid, green mould on their limbs. All are dead but one man,—it is you! But years, though so slowly they come, have then scathed you. There is the coming of age on your brow, and the will is relaxed in the cells of the brain. Still that will, though enfeebled, exceeds all that man knew before you; through the will you live on, gnawed with famine. And nature no longer obeys you in that death-spreading region; the sky is a sky of iron, and the air has iron clamps, and the ice-rocks wedge in the ship. Hark how it cracks and groans! Ice will imbed it as amber imbeds a straw. And a man has gone forth, living yet, from the ship and its dead; and he has clambered up the spikes of an iceberg, and the two moons gaze down on his form. That man is yourself, and terror is on you,—terror; and terror has swallowed up your will. And I see, swarming up the steep ice-rock, gray, grizzly things. The bears of the North have scented their quarry; they come near you and nearer, shambling, and rolling their bulk. And in that day every moment shall seem to you longer than the centuries through which you have passed. And heed this: after life, moments continued make the bliss or the hell of eternity."

"Hush," said the whisper. "But the day, you assure me, is far off, very far! I go back to the almond and rose of Damascus! Sleep!"

The room swam before my eyes. I became insensible. When I recovered, I found G—— holding my hand and smiling. He said, "You, who have always declared yourself proof against mesmerism, have succumbed at last to my friend Richards."

"Where is Mr. Richards?"

"Gone, when you passed into a trance, saying quietly to me, 'Your friend will not wake for an hour.'"

I asked, as collectedly as I could, where Mr. Richards lodged.

"At the Trafalgar Hotel."

"Give me your arm," said I to G——. "Let us call on him; I have something to say."

When we arrived at the hotel, we were told that Mr. Richards had returned twenty minutes before, paid his bill, left directions with his servant (a Greek) to pack his effects, and proceed to Malta by the steamer that should leave Southampton the next day. Mr. Richards had merely said of his own movements, that he had visits to pay in the neighborhood of London, and it was uncertain whether he should be able to reach Southampton in time for that steamer; if not, he should follow in the next one.

The waiter asked me my name. On my informing him, he gave me a note that Mr. Richards had left for me, in case I called.

The note was as follows:—

"I wished you to utter what was in your mind. You obeyed. I have therefore established power over you. For three months from this day you can communicate to no living man what has passed between us. You cannot even show this note to the friend by your side. During three months, silence complete as to me and mine. Do you doubt my power to lay on you this command? try to disobey me. At the end of the third month the spell is raised. For the rest, I spare you. I shall visit your grave a year and a day after it has received you."

So ends this strange story, which I ask no one to believe. I write it down exactly three months after I received the above note. I could not write it before, nor could I show to G——, in spite of his urgent request, the note which I read under the gas-lamp by his side.

D'OUTRE MORT.
BY HARRIET PRESCOTT SPOFFORD.

A MOUNTAIN intervale all velveted in green, and half the verdure overlaid with gold by broad rays of sunset falling level through the pass,— the hills, behind, a gray and gloomy encampment softened with wreaths of vapor and dim recesses of deepest purple, and here and there above the gaps a pale star trembling on the paler blue. In spite of the approaching night, there was a gay glad strength about the scene, so that all who saw it might have felt light at heart, as if the rocky rampart shut out the sorrows of the world and made the charmed valley an enchanted place.

They had been mowing in the intervale; half-formed haycocks, picturesquely piled along the meadows, loaded the air with heavy sweetness; in one, partly overthrown, a lounger lolled luxuriously, singing idly to himself that little Venetian song of Browning's, to some tune delightful as the words:—

"O, which were best, to roam or rest?
The land's lap or the water's breast?
To sleep on yellow millet-sheaves,
Or swim in lucid shallows, just
Eluding water-lily leaves,
An inch from Death's black fingers thrust
To lock you, whom release he must;
Which life were best on summer eves?"

The perfumed wind blew softly over the singer, like a placid breath; the sense of gathering evening hung above him; he lay upon the billowy hay as if it were a cloud; he was a voluptuary in his pleasures; well for him if they were always as innocent.

A young girl approached the singer, swinging her hat as she came, and radiant in the low sunshine.

She was named Orient,—either because she seemed, with her golden locks, her fresh fair tints, like an impersonation of morning and the East, or because when she was born hope's day-star rose again in her mother's forlorn heart. Such a lovely yet half-fantastic creature was she, that you hardly believed in her existence when away from her.

"What are you looking for, Orient?" said the lounger.

"The fountain of youth," answered her silvery tones. "It should be somewhere in this happy valley."

"You do not need it," he replied after a lingering glance.

She stooped and extricated a long sweetbrier bough from the hay with which it had been bent but not cut down, and twisted it, still blossoming, round and round her head till it made a fragrant diadem of rosy stars.

"Do not," said Reymund. "Take it off; or I shall have to do as Voltaire did: erect my long, thin body and stand before you like a point of admiration!"

Orient did not reply; and, fulfilling his threat, he went on by her side to the old farm-house that had been turned into a summer hostelry for guests. More stars were beginning to steal forth in the tender firmament; the breeze blew down more freshly from the hills and brought the big dews and scattered starbeams with it; music was hushed, and all the world was still. It was summer evening, yet an unreal kind of summer, as summer might be in a distant dream, blown over by cool, awakening winds. Now and then Orient stopped to pick up a great butterfly that had fallen benumbed from its perch and lay it gently to rest among the leaves, without brushing a speck of dust from its freckled wings; after that her fingers worked in a vine by the way, and she pulled aside a tendril that kept a sleepy flower from shutting up its petals. As she did so, a little mother-bird upon her eggs stirred and briefly twittered out her secret to Orient's ear. Reymund, who loitered in waiting for her, thought she seemed, as much as any of them, like a flower, a moth, a bird herself, a beautiful and almost dumb existence of nature.

He was not a man easily intimidated, or of unvaried experience; but the thin atmosphere of awe about this girl was something he had never penetrated; the ease with which he met another, toward her became impertinence; gay and careless with many, he felt that she was something apart, sacred as a passion-flower; he scarcely dared approach her lightly; when he spoke to her he crossed himself in his heart.

They had never met until a month ago, yet their address had been familiar almost from the first; on her side, through a large-eyed, childlike fearlessness; on his—he could not have answered why. He watched her as one watches a clear planet glow steadily from the soft, golden sky, but he seemed nevertheless to know all her characteristics without studying them,—he imagined that to one weary of trifle and artifice and the hollow way of the world, here was the rest divine. Yet beyond a point, he found this cool, remote being inaccessible,—as though there had been a gulf between them. He knew not how to call the blush to her cheek, the sparkle to her eye; if she had been some alien creature she might have been nearer,—to enrich her with human love was as fruitless an effort as scattering the pollen of a rose into the heart of a cold white lily. And yet, Reymund knew—as if through the same natural operations as those by which his pulse was made to beat, his breath to draw—that Orient's soul needed his for its entireness; that his soul required hers, all as much as a star needed its atmosphere, a flower its fragrance, the earth itself its spheral roundness. It was not so much that he already loved her passionately, as that he felt himself lost without her; he had been in Orient's presence, it seemed, all the time that he had ever lived; how could he then depart from it? If that which was a clod suddenly found itself a bed of blossom, how could it ever return again to dreary earthiness?

He watched her now approaching. Had any one said that she trailed lustre behind her as she walked, he would have answered that he had seen it. But to speak to her of any grace or charm or perfection that she possessed,— why, these things were herself, her identity, sacred and secret; as easily to some skyey messenger of solemn heaven commend his airy flight!

"In what wonderful ways these mountains change their expression!" said Reymund, as she joined him again at last.

"Yes," she replied, "they are different beings every hour."

"A little while ago," he continued, "they seemed like an army of giants sitting down to besiege the valley; now they are a wall between us and mankind; death cannot break through it, sickness cannot cross it."

"They are more alive than that," said Orient. "This old sombre one moved aside just now to make room for the little alp laughing over his shoulder, with the rosy vapor streaming high on her face."

"Perhaps you hear what they are saying to one another, then?" he asked, half jestingly.

"I often do."

"And you will translate?"

"No. In the first place you would laugh; in the last place disbelieve."

"On my soul—no!"

"I am not certain that you have a soul."

"Indeed? Is it so?" half sadly.

"They say what the torrents rushing down by Chamouni say!"

"Ah! And at other times?"

"They talk of the beginning of the earth, and conjecture concerning the end of things."

"And do they take any notice of you? Nature always seems to me careless and indifferent."

"They invite me to come up and lie down on their great sides where the sun has lain all day before me. Yes, they always smile upon me."

"Do not go,—at least until the mamma and I go with you."

"I should not be afraid alone."

No,—fear had never found the depths of those liquid, lucent eyes, he thought. "The mountains might be civil enough," he rejoined, "and give you their purple berries to eat, their wild white brooks to drink; but I could not answer for the black bears and snakes."

"I think I could."

"And this, of course, is only what you interpret the hills to mean, sitting there in their grim conclave and affording us such a narrow coronal of sky?" asked Reymund, smiling.

"I do not know," she answered doubtfully. "I said things were real to me."

"There must have been those like you, who first saw and believed in fairies and all the goblin people," he said, still smiling.

"My father died before I was born," said Orient. "Perhaps that gave me some lien upon the spiritual world."

"Then you see bogles as well as other things,—as well as the personalities of bud and bird and granite pile? Uncanny creature! What pleasure shall I take in meeting your glance when it rests also on a dead man behind me, and on the fetch of one about to join the innumerable caravan beside me? I must take my revenge normally and in kind,—if I die before you, you shall surely have a visitation from me. How should you like that?"

"You would be just as welcome then as now," she answered gravely.

"An equivocal compliment. Nevertheless, I accept it as a challenge. Will you promise its counterpart?"

"When I die," said Orient, "I shall have other things to do."

"But I would like to see a ghost, just to be assured that there are such things."

"As if there could be any doubt!"

"You understand, then," he said, as she went in under the low woodbine-curtained door, "that at some time—when time shall be no more—I will cast my shadow at your feet!"

It was an hour later that, while he still strolled in the short, wet grass and enjoyed the rich, half-dusky atmosphere, he heard Orient singing gently from her window, as she leaned out upon the cool, star-sown air, and the song seemed to belong to her, like a natural expression, as to the night the night-wind, or to the dark the dew:—

"In the evening over me leaning,
Often I fancy a waving wing,
And with the warning of blushing morning
Softly glimmers the same fair thing.

"O bright being, beyond the seeing
Of aught but the spirit that feels you near,
Your white star leaving, and earthward cleaving,
You break the murk of this mortal sphere.

"Still, sweet stranger, in peace or danger,
Out of the air above me bloom,
And heaven's own sweetness in such completeness
Drop on my head from your shining plume!"
Even while he heard her singing, the sense of her remoteness gave
Reymund a slight shudder. If she had been one shade more human; if he
had ever seen her moved by any sparkle of wit, any drollery of humor, into
a frolicking outburst of laughter, by any mischievous vexation into a flash
of anger, a season of pettishness,—but no, such little incidents affected her
no more than thistle-down affects the wind; and, recognizing it, Reymund
knew that he loved her, yet felt somehow as he felt who had pledged a
bridal ring upon the finger of a ghost; as that youth felt, perchance, whose
beautiful mistress was after all a ghoul. He need not have concerned
himself; Orient had no especial care for him; he passed before her, busy in
her world of dreams, like a shadow; if she smiled upon him, it was as she
smiled on everything else about her, as she smiled on the pink-wreathed
peach-bough, on the urchin tumbling in grass, on the sunbeam overlaying
both, on blue sky or on rainy weather; though, indeed, for the latter, Orient
had superfluous smiles; she was always sunny herself upon a stormy day;
she used to say that it seemed as if Nature had grown so familiar with her
that she could afford to receive her and show herself to her in undress.
Perhaps, had Reymund been more free himself from the soil and stain of
earth, Orient would not have been so intangible.

They were going one day up the mountain, Orient, her mother, the guide, and Reymund, the first two riding, Reymund and the guide on foot. The air was so clear that it seemed like living in the inside of a crystal; everything stood with sharp outlines, as if drawn with a burin upon the deep substance of the blue: far away tender gauzes took up the distance, but that was merely on the outside edges of the world. After they had exhausted the view from the wide-reaching summit, where the eye seemed to wrest from the Creator more than had ever been given to it, they went below into the shelter of the great rocks and lunched. It was late in the afternoon ere they remounted and sought their way down the long descent. The path which had been slight with difficulties in climbing was now full of downward terrors. Orient bent far back in her seat, unable to see where her horse would plant his feet. It seemed to her that he was stepping over sheer abysses, and just as she herself went sliding and slipping forward over his head and down, a strong arm from an unseen form behind the cliff, round which she had just wound, would grasp her, and Reymund would hold her firm till the beast stood four-square again. It was to her a thing like the arm of Providence made visible to faith. Suddenly the girth broke, and but for that strong arm on the instant outstretched, Providence itself alone knows what would have become of her. Reymund caught her then as she reeled from the saddle, and placed her on the ground. The horse, startled by the unexpectedness of the affair, fled forward; the guide left the bridle he had held behind and pursued him. Catching the rein with a jerk and oath, he dealt such a blow with his boot that the animal lost his balance and fell, and would have rolled over the precipice but for a prostrate tree. In a moment what Reymund had wanted to see was granted him. Orient sprang forward, her face aflame, her eyes like balefires. The guide, amazed, as one might be at the sight of an avenger in his path, obeyed her single word, her vehement gesture, and plunged down the way and left them.

"Orient! what have you done?" cried her mother.

"Well, well, mamma," answered the suddenly convicted and penitent one, "we can follow his red cap."

But the guide, twice too cunning, hid himself in underhung paths that he knew, and they had not a sign or signal for aid.

Nevertheless, Reymund gladly accepted this fate because of the thing that brought it, and at which another man would have looked askance. This thing, this little temper, had proved to him that Orient was human,—and, therefore, to be won. He raised the pony, remounted Orient, and did his best in place of their faithless leader, trusting more to the instincts of the animals themselves than to any mountain-craft of his own.

The sharp outlines of distant peaks began to burn and blacken, those of the nearer rock and stunted shrub to grow diffuse; the air was keen and chill, a reddening sunset smouldered in clouds below them and shut out the world, a cold, wet mist below threatened to come creeping up around them. The horses neighed to each other, grew jaded and uncertain, stopped. Masses of impassable rock closed them in on every side, save the narrow defile through which they came and the precipice below; the atmosphere was purple with shade and clung to them in dew; already one star hung out its blue lamp.

"We can go no farther," said Reymund. "This spot is more sheltered than any we are likely to find. Let us do what we can for comfort, and wait for the morning."

The mother bewailed herself; but Orient made cheer, and while Reymund corralled the horses, she was busy collecting twigs and splinters and bits of wood and dry moss in a pile. "Light them with your matches, Reymund," she said. "A cigar will keep you warm, but we need a bit of blaze, perhaps."

"When it is darker," he replied; "you will need it more a little nearer to the witching time."

"Do you imagine we shall see witches?"

"Take care, or you will see stars."

"He rode alone through the silent night,
She swam like a star to his left and right,"

sang Orient. "After all, it is not the Walpurgis Night."

"If we could only have a cup of tea!" sighed the mamma, at a loss for her luxuries in the wilderness.

"It will be so much more refreshing to-morrow," said Orient. "And seasoned with romance,—a dash of danger,—your first adventure, little mother!"

But the little mother had no fancy for adventures; and while her daughter lost all her serenity and was crazy with delight at the wild beauty of the thing, she grew more and more lachrymose, and afforded at last a good background of shower for all Orient's rainbows. Thereon Orient, sitting down, put her arms round her and comforted her, till the mother became herself somewhat alive to the circumstance that one seldom saw such a scene twice in a lifetime.

They had remained on the rocky platform where they paused, a shelf that after a few yards ended in an abrupt fall that led away by a course of stark precipices into the great valley beneath. This valley, filled with rolling vapor, whose volumes, smitten by sunset, were fused in splendid color, made a pavilion of cloud beneath them where billows of fleecy crimson and shining scarlet curdled together into creamy crests, here seeming to lash in feather-white foam against the base of some crag, and there letting a late sunbeam plough through spaces of a violet-dark drift till they were all inwrought with gold. Above them the cold and mighty heaven was already faintly but thickly strewn with stars.

"Into what awful and glorious region are we translated!" cried Orient. "We are above the world and the people of the world. Are we flesh and blood?"

"The free spirits of the air 'have no such liberty' as this of ours," said Reymund.

"It is just as if we were dead!" shivered the mamma. "And I'm sure it's cold enough for that!"

Orient wrapped the shawls about the doleful little woman, while Reymund opened his knapsack for any remnants of lunch that might afford them consolation. He kindled the fire, too, for the colors were fading away beneath, and the sky was getting gloomy overhead; and, warmed and enlivened in the genial light of the briefly crackling blaze, they forgot that they were lost upon the mountain, and all the possible horrors of their fate. But to Reymund there were few horrors in it, for if he died of exposure and starvation there on the bald, pitiless mountain, it would be with Orient in his arms at last.

While the fire crackled, Reymund found in his breast-pocket a tiny flask of cordial which he divided into three portions. "Drink it," he said to them, "and make it take the place of the tea. It is Chartreuse—oily sunshine—distilled from the cones of some old fir-tree. First cousin to the cedars of Lebanon, for all I know. Mark how you taste hemlock in it. Socrates poisoned with hemlock? No, no; he drank himself to death on Chartreuse."

Orient heard him indignantly. "I do not like it," said she, when her turn came, and left hers in the horn. Reymund laughed; he hesitated a moment, then tossed it off himself.

The fire did not last them long, for all the twigs they could collect were scanty; the blaze had heated the rock a little; they drew closer to it, and the mother, curling up against it in her shawls, composed herself as she could for slumber; the voices of Orient and Reymund, from where they still sat and talked together, lulled her as the murmur of the waterfall lulled Sleep himself. Orient was repeating Jean Ingelow's dream of her lover fallen and dead among the hills, with its vague and awesome imagery. "I do not understand," she said, as she ceased, "this solicitude that my mother and so many others feel concerning their burial-place. I love life, delicious life; but if we die and lie unburied here forever among the lonely precipices, it will not matter any more to us than it did to the youth." And she repeated again:—

"The first hath no advantage,—it shall not soothe his slumber
That a lock of his brown hair his father aye shall keep;
For the last, he nothing grudgeth, it shall naught his quiet cumber
That in a golden mesh of *his*, callow eaglets sleep."
Reymund quaked at the moment, as he thought of any lustrous lock of Orient's curling out of the fierce beak that should tear it away from the white brow. Then he said: "Too philosophic by half. As for me, with the first peep of day in this high meridian, I shall be up and doing, and find a way to our level again or—perish in the attempt."

"Resolved to perish, any way. Give you liberty or give you death. *I* do not feel in such a hurry to be gone. How silent and solemn it is,—what a clear darkness,—listen a moment and catch the sough of that pine forest far beneath, like the wings of some great spirit sifting the air. I have never been so near heaven. I understand now why in the Bible they so often withdrew into a high mountain."

Reymund did not answer her. "Say your prayers, innocent one," was what he thought. "Wherever you are, there heaven is near."

By and by Orient crept closer to her mother for mutual comfort, wound her own cloak round her like a chrysalis, and drowsed and dreamed.

Reymund sat beside her, his knees drawn up, his hands clasped round them. It was very cool; the air was so still that he wondered at the absence of a stinging frost, and he hugged himself thus for warmth. Orient stirred in her half-recumbent sleep, and her head fell on his shoulder. After that the solid mountain was less immovable than he. He let the beautiful head remain, watching it with downcast, sidelong gaze; if he had longed with all his heart to smooth one tress, to put his arm over her in a sheltering embrace, he dared not touch her. Something said to him that she was of a grade above, as the disembodied is beyond the clay; said, too, that whatever lovely or fine there might be in himself, the thickness of the outer wrapping rendered it invisible to her; that for Orient to read him right he must wait for another life. In spite of all that, he hoped,—hoped madly and wildly, there in the chill night, with the beautiful head fallen on his shoulder and the sweet, warm breath stealing gently across his bending brow. He had a strange fancy now and then that out of the encircling shadow a great face came and looked,—whether that of some uncreated thing, some phantasm of his brain, or that of some celestial being, some resident of vast spaces, or only a wild beast, a big, brown bear, roving on their tracks and coming to peer about their unprotected bivouac. Whatever it was, it retired as often as it came, awed in its turn, he thought, by the sweet innocence of that golden head. A late moon rose down over the low side of the earth as he still sat there; he knew it by the strange coppery light that began to glow through the vapors that yet filled the gulfs beneath, and boil them to a scum of dark, dun gold; then at last a broad beam parted the tumbling and sulphurous fogs, and the bright, thin crescent of the waning moon cut itself out on a clear air behind the horn of the hill, and, as if swinging from its sharp cusp, hung the watery diamond of the morning star. Still Reymund did not lift the head from his shoulder; he chose rather that the fair apparition of daybreak at this height above the earth might happen to him, as if through the imposition of that dear and tender touch. By and by she stirred restlessly,— the spell of her slumber was breaking; he moved away gently and left her the rock for a pillow. When the heavens were paling and retreating in a mist of star-breath, and when all the world was whitening about her and the great floor of cloud beneath was inwrought by dawn with sparks of fire, so that they seemed wrapped in an atmosphere of flame and snow, Orient awoke.

No hero in his self-restraint, in one wild, forgetful moment of that morning, Reymund told Orient that he loved her.

She repulsed him so gently that it gave him reason to hope, yet so firmly that he could do nothing but despair.

He urged that she was unconscious of herself, that she did not know her own heart, nor what it wanted; that he had approached her inner life more nearly than another might ever do; that, give him time and chance, he could not fail to win her.

She only answered that she was not won.

Before, in their windings and wanderings, they had reached the foot of the mountain that day, they met their recusant and repentant guide coming up with others in search of them, and all their toil and trouble were over.

Reymund's holiday was over too. He was to return next day to his home, to engagements previously formed and not to be disregarded.

"At least," he said to Orient, not sadly, but with a certain vigor of intention in his tone, "you will allow me to visit you at your mother's house?"

"You could not do a kinder thing," answered Orient, feeling now the gap that he would leave, and which nothing could quite fill, and willing to grant him anything but what he most desired.

"Then you will see me on Saturdays."

"Every Saturday!" she exclaimed, with a bright face that made his heart bound. "That is too much to ask."

"Of you, perhaps; not of me. Sunday is a spare day; if I use it for God's worship, it shall be at what shrine I please,—St. Orient's or another's."

"And it is such a long ride," demurred she, remembering the miles on miles of low sea-coast country threaded with rivers and inlaid with marshes, that he must cross, all day flying along through their damp breath and salt winds. "Nine hours; I am afraid I ought not to allow it. And yet,—and yet, nine or nineteen, it shall make no difference."

Orient had hesitated in her last sentence, wondering how she could deny herself the sympathy in her little pursuits that through this time she had received from Reymund. She had not encountered it before; it was delightful to her; perhaps it only had not taught her love because she did not know what love was. She had but little knowledge of human nature, almost none at all of her own nature: she preferred natural religion before theology, natural history, with its grandiose revolutions, before the petty struggles of warriors and diplomatists which her view was not broad enough to throw into epochs and revolutions more grandiose yet: it was Reymund who had taught her to look with kindly curiosity upon the lives of those about her, in hopes, it may be, of teaching her at last to look in upon her own. Of that she was unaware; but the interest in the flower never found before to-day, the discovery of the bird whose note had ravished the ear last sunset, the hunt up brookside and hill for a fragment of quartz that should have a mountain range and outlying spurs of amethyst crystals, or one full of imbedded beryls, the shining hexagons like drops of light filtered through seawater, or any heap of blooded garnets, a blaze of concrete color; the search into the age of the old pine-tree on the precipice; into the mountain strata, and the wonderment concerning that day of the earth's date on which they were upheaved; the tracing out the path of some glacier with all its ancient and icy terrors overgrown by the verdant moss and turf of the moraine; the perpetual looking for the Maker's fingers in his work,—all this, and such as this, she would miss and must resign if she forbade those recurring Saturdays. And then, on the other hand, a friend to meet with the results of work, the choice book, the week's research, its thought, its fancy: she who had had no intimates, few friends—

Reymund did not wait for her to balance her ideas.

"The train arrives," said he, "by five o'clock,—a little before. Every Saturday, therefore, at five o'clock, I shall be in your drawing-room."

The thing was settled, then, without her. She began all at once to fear that, after all, it would not happen so; he would let other things creep between;

when he was fairly at a distance from her he would be angry with her for having quite failed to feel that entire satisfaction in him, to give him that love which, in a high ideal, she believed to be due from every woman to her husband; a thousand things would hinder.

"I can hardly believe it," she said.

"I am too happy when you doubt it," he replied, half reading her thoughts. "It gives me hope; for we can easily believe that to which we are indifferent. How can I be hindered when I will it,—and when you wish it?" The blush that streamed up her temples doubly pleased him. "Do not doubt it!" he exclaimed, with more vivacity than so small a thing appeared to demand. "For, see, I swear it! I will be with you on each Saturday at five o'clock, with your permission, until the day I die!"

So, dropping her hand, he went down the lane to the coach. But, looking back, he saw her still standing in the doorway, hung with such drooping drapery of woodbine round her head, the sunlight lying in a glory on her golden hair, the downy bloom upon her cheek as though it were a peach, a smile upon her lip, and heaven's own blue within her eye,—she seemed the incarnation of a summer sunrise. He saw the riotous wind lift one curl and twine it with the next, drop the petal of a rose upon her mouth, kiss and kiss again her ivory forehead, free and welcome where he dared not venture,—and the love in his heart made the blood boil hotly up his veins to cheek and brow,—and for all testimony to his thrilling passion, he only cried, "Every Saturday, at five o'clock!" and was away.

But before Reymund plunged afresh into the exterior world, which, for these weeks, had been shut from his sight, he turned aside for one last outlook upon pleasure. Thus it happened that he left the train at an earlier station than the one near Orient's home, partly to avoid recognition in the future, partly for the sake of mounting and subduing a spirited horse which had been brought up to tear himself into a foam at sight of the engine. Reymund meant to gratify himself that day with a stroll through Orient's garden and among the haunts of her bright youth. No one would have taken him for anything but an apparition, who saw him galloping down the long country roads in a cloud of dust. When he had conquered the angry temper of the beast he abated his gait and paced slowly along the margin of the twice-mown meadows, splendid in noon sunshine, over the shaven surfaces of rusty reds and browns, into which they shaded all their gilded verdure. Now and then a bittern cried from the bank of a tiny thread of the tide, other notes were hushed, there was only to be heard through the wide midday air the unbroken treble of the crickets, across which the rich horns of the locusts shrilled like the elfin trumpets of a summer's state. Reymund hitched his horse, found a penetrable portion of the garden paling, and entered.

It was a large, old garden, laid out, fifty years ago, perhaps, in a kind of pleasance; for in one place a slight hill rose above the rest, while paths wandered round it into new and unsuspected regions; in another a brook meandered and sang silverly over shining pebbles, and among arrow-heads and lily-pods, and, dallying, went its way at last to empty into some tide-streak and find the sounding sea that called to it all night. Weeds, of course, had overgrown the beds, the untrained grapes hung heavily from wall and trellis, wasps and blackbirds made merry together with the nectar of ripening pears, plum and peach dropped ungathered from the bough; vine and tendril, leaf and spray, and branch and blossom, all wrought themselves to a delicious tangle of perfume and rustle and color. Here, through the beautiful and envious weeds, a gladiolus reared his flames, a larkspur absorbed the very blue, a carnation scattered spice; here honeysuckles still blew out a perfect fragrance, while mourning-brides and gillyflowers and spiked lavender and pansies sowed the air with their old-fashioned sweetness. The soft, lonely sky stretched away over the garden and the meadows to haze itself round low and distant woods, and all the empty air seemed sad and desolate between,—the fulness and richness of life at its high noon touching close upon the anti-climax of desert solitude. Through the place a light east-wind was blowing that had in it a tonic for the lungs like the sparkle of champagne. And, somehow, through all the spaces of the neglected garden the spell of Orient seemed complete. There Orient must have stood to twine that white rose upon the porch; there her fingers must have twinkled among the young vine-leaves; there, on that bank of turf, she must many an afternoon have sat at work; there, in the shallow crystal of the brook, she had waded with white feet to set the water-plants. These lichen-covered apple-trees had shed, how many a springtime, the rosy snow of their petals around her head; these gnarled old bergamots had dropped their pulpy globes into her hands; this nut-tree put out its leaves on the day when she was born; her little feet had worn these paths. The garden was the shadow of Orient herself, reduced to dumb and to material things. He wondered what it would be by the magic of moonlight,—the whole place silvered over with tranquil sheen, and raised from every day's dull sight into the dreamy and ideal,—full of cool dew, and silence, and holy hush, as if it waited on her white sleep. Just under his feet, where the seed had been thrown in handfuls, he traced, written out with blue forget-me-nots, the name of Orient.

It would not do for him to stay much longer here; he should grow wild with hopes and fancies, for all he knew, tread out that lovely name with his heel. She must, she should be won! He clutched a cluster of the forget-me-nots, quickly escaped the labyrinth, galloped back to the station at a rate that streaked his chafing steed,—and so away from dreams to life and real work.

Thus Reymund returned to his routine; bills and lawsuits and politics, routes and rides; they were not calculated to lift him to any higher level than the old one.

And Orient and her mother came home; the mother having made quite as close acquaintance with the mountains as she cared to do.

Saturdays, now, surely as they came, brought Reymund under the same roof with Orient. Perhaps in their brief indulgence he found pardon for all the sins of the week,—for the week had its sins, its little trivial condoning of misdemeanors as unimportant, matters which lower one as steadily and certainly over the great pit, as block and tackle might do over another. On Sunday nights, when he glided away in the outward train, he felt as if it were an easy thing to maintain the height which, by Orient's side, he gained; but after a Monday morning on the exchange, after a Tuesday night in the salon, after his evening gallop on the horse possessed with the spirit of Satan, he said to himself, "It is of no use. Nature is too crude in me, too gross a strain, too deep a dye. I should be like Shelley's rock in the black abyss, that

'Has from unimaginable years
Sustained itself with terror and with toil
Over a gulf, and, with the agony
With which it clings, seems slowly coming down.'

The thing is to abandon." Yet Saturday's sunset shone for him again always over Orient's garden.

He had come one evening and found Orient among the grape-vines, playing with a parcel of little children, as pretty, bright, and fresh as a bunch of flowers. After the hubbub of business, the dust of travel, this garden, in a far outlying city suburb stretching towards the sea, seemed as pure and innocent as Eden. On Sunday morning, when the air soared illumined with a stiller lustre, when the azure deepened as if fresh-washed by sacred rains and dews, when the winds bore no murmur but that of ripening leaf and floating petal, when the birds themselves seemed to sing in the Sabbath, and all the wide world to be gladly and tranquilly conscious of the day,— they went to church together. If Orient was rapt in the worship, Reymund was at an exaltation as high for him,—rapt in his worship of her. By times this very thing lifted him into the upper region, his soul rose buoyant on the prayer and praise, and floated forward like a waif on the full tide of the organ's music. When, afterward, he found himself and his sentience again, he said the thing was in him,—could he but keep the pitch,—were Orient forever by him to give him that key-note. But alone we come into this world, alone we go out of it. Neither Orient nor another could, for all eternity, give the tone to any soul; that discord or that harmony which one shall make must be the result of one's own being.

He sat with Orient, in the afternoon, on the bank of turf that sloped down to the clear, brown brook, in whose bed many a diving and dipping sunbeam wrought mosaics of light and shade with the shining pebbles. The brook rustled and lilted on its way, a bird above it turned its burden into melody, now and then a waft of wind rippled all its course till the lily leaves shivered and turned up their crimson linings, soft clouds chased one another across the sky,—everything around wore the bloom of peace and pleasure.

"I often fear," said Reymund, "that I must come here no more. The place grows too dear for one that must some day leave it."

Orient turned and looked at him. He saw her tremble. "Not come here any more!" she said.

"Ah, Orient!" he cried, "once I declared to you the purpose of my life. Sometimes—now—sometimes—it seems to me as if you were almost won."

He bent above her, glowing and passionate and daring. She trembled again, neither drew away, nor surrendered herself to the waiting grasp.

"I do not know," she answered him, the globy tears suffusing her eyes till each one shone like the great star that hung its blue lamp in the zenith that night when they were lost upon the mountain. "Perhaps I cannot read my heart; but does a woman really love that which is less strong than herself? I must lean upon my husband, not he on me."

"Am I so weak?" asked Reymund, with some bitterness, and a quiver on his lip. "Consider. If your own nature had been invested with a coarser flesh, left out thereby to coarser temptations,—since passions are things of the flesh,—what would have come of it? Then, if thrown in the midst of the revel, loving the flash of merriment, the excitement of chance, and wine and dice were going round—But, no! such speech is profanity. Yet, Orient, under all habit, under all action, I think there is that in my soul akin to yours, made to rule it and absorb it, hidden by the body; but there,—made to be loved by you, as you, all of you, flaws and beauties, are loved by me!"

"If I could only *see* your soul," said Orient, half yielding, contrite, yet uncertain.

"One day perhaps you will," answered Reymund, his repeater giving the hour to his finger-pressure. "Now I must go."

He rose, stooped again and touched her smooth, cold forehead with his mouth. The touch sent the blood back to his heart. "With time," he murmured. "O, with time! she shall yet—she shall! Good by,—till Saturday again at five o'clock!" and then was gone.

All that week Reymund walked through his work with an absent mind, as if his spirit had half left his body, disengaging itself from the automaton of bone and muscle, as one might say; abstracted and lost in his thoughts, his wishes, his absolute resolutions. Old haunts had no attraction for him, old faces brought him no satisfaction, he sought no pleasure but such as was to be found on the back of that horse possessed by the spirit of Satan. And so he existed till the sunrise of Saturday, when, before it should be quite time for the train, he had the horse brought round for a gallop, as if he would ride the wind and tame the whirlwind.

In the mean time Orient pursued her way in what, for her, was perturbation. There seemed to be a riddle in these days beyond her reading. Penitent over her pride in presuming herself to be stronger than her lover, conscious that she could not dispense with him, yet full as sure that she felt no perfect passion for him, there was nothing to do but marvel what it meant. "I am drawn to him," she said to herself. "Ah, I know that well enough! But have I any right to be? If there were something to confirm me! If I thought the good and beautiful part were any abiding principle, were anything but love of me! If I could only see his soul!"

She was walking that Saturday afternoon in the woods that could be seen from her garden across the meadows. It was a clear October afternoon, the red leaves were dropping round her and leaving the bright blue sky more bare with every gentle gust that brought them to her feet; a bracing day of early autumn, when the wind fainted with the sweet freight of balsam from the pines, and all things only prophesied hope and lightsomeness. In spite of this, Orient could not tell why she had a constant sensation of gray and misty horizons, of marshy air and cold sea-wind all day; as she walked now, the fitful breeze in the tree-tops seemed the muffled murmur of waves on the distant beach, and once in a while she shivered as if a cold foam-wreath were flying by her face. She thought at first that all this damp and drear sensation was some sympathy with Reymund, now travelling along the sea-coast on his way to her. "But what absurdity!" she said. "Where the track lies, the sky is as blue as this one; the wind is scarcely more chilly there than here. Reymund is rolling along, comfortable among his cushions and books; and not a naked spirit all abroad in the sea-scented air!"

She went home on the causeway that was laid along the meadows,—hurrying a little, for she judged by the sinking sun that it must be nearly time for the arrival of the train. As she went, she heard her name called.

She turned, for the voice seemed to come from the woods. But seeing no one, she fancied the note of some bird had followed her.

Again the sound. Her name; and Reymund's voice. "He has come," thought Orient, with a thrill of unsuspected pleasure, "and he is calling me from the garden." And she made all haste to answer the summons in person. Going along, then, with her boughs of bright leaves, she wished she had not delayed so long in the woods,—her dress so soiled, and her hands, her hair so disordered; she resolved to steal in at the side door and freshen her toilet before greeting him. As the door was opened to her, "Mr. Reymund has come," said the maid, gleefully. "I have just let him in. He is waiting in the drawing-room."

"Very well," answered Orient. "Tell him I will be there directly."

She hastened towards the staircase, boughs in hand.

"You haven't seen your friend?" asked her aunt, passing her on the landing as she sped up.

"No," replied Orient again; "have you?"

"I just met him in the hall as he was entering the drawing-room," said the good woman, calling over the balusters and going her way.

Orient hurried at her bath, clad herself with all despatch, and put on a garment whose airy frills and ruffles made her look like a white rose. As she went by her mother's room, the mother looked out and said, lightly, "Reymund has come. Did you know it?"

"Yes, mamma," she answered. "Why didn't you go and make him welcome?"

"O, my hair was all down!" said the other. "I just caught a glimpse of him, passing the foot of the stairs as he went into the drawing-room."

So Orient stepped slowly down, adjusting her bracelets as she went. She saw Reymund a second, as the winding way of the stairs for that space allowed her, standing in the bay-window and looking out. She did not know what made her so hesitate to enter. She paused a moment longer in the doorway, gazing in.

The room was very gay with bunches of deep-blue and scarlet salvia, and drooping clusters of barberry boughs stringing their splendid pendants all along most graceful curves; but there was another brightness than that in the room. It was where Reymund stood in the embrasure of the window, with the late sunlight falling all over him. She wondered that he did not advance to meet her; but, as she wondered, went up the room toward him.

"Something must have happened to make him very happy," thought Orient. "I never saw such a smile!"

Perhaps it was this smile that so transfigured him; a plain man commonly, the sunshine now seemed to bring out rich, dark tints on the countenance, the eyes overflowed with light, and whether it were grace of posture, overlying sunshine, or beaming smile, features and face and figure expressed a subtle harmony, and the man was beautiful,—beautiful as a strong angel pictured in some instant of stooping flight.

"He does not mean to speak till I do," thought Orient again.

But as she drew near, the smile changed to a look of utter melancholy, as a shining cloud melts into rain,—a melancholy gaze that pierced her through and through. She put out her hand, nevertheless, to take his extended grasp.

And there was nothing there!

In the same instant, with a loud and terrible voice, crying, "Orient!"—a voice as if it were the voice of death, the tomb, and all corruption,—the thing had vanished; the place was empty!

That cry rang through the house, that loud and terrible voice. Maid and mother rushed into the room; and they found no one there but Orient, fallen unconscious to the floor.

It did not take long to revive the child. "Something has happened to Reymund," she said, upon lifting her head. "We must go to him at once!"

"My love!" cried her mother. "The idea of the thing. The—"

But expostulations were wasted breath; while they were being made, Orient was calmly getting on her travelling-gown, and, seeing herself powerless, the mother—with her heart palpitating in the ends of her fingers through awe and through alarm, and interweaving with the ejaculations that escaped her chattering teeth a thousand instructions to her quaking maid and sister—hastened to do likewise and be off with her.

Thus it happened that the telegram from Reymund's brother crossed the travellers on their way; and they reached his brother's house in the gray of the shivering morning.

It was just as Orient's heart had told her. Reymund had been thrown from his horse on the previous morning, striking his head on a curbstone's edge; he had been taken up senseless, and had lain since then in a stupor only broken by his twice calling her name in the afternoon. At a little after five o'clock he had risen on the pillow, and in a loud and terrible voice had called Orient again, and then had fallen back; and whether he were dead or alive there was no one able to say.

Orient threw off her hat and shawl and stole into the apartment where Reymund had been placed. The white face that fastened her eye was still as a mask of clay, and there was stamped upon it that look of unutterable melancholy into which she had seen the smile fade yesterday,—the linen where it lay was less white, a marble image had been less still. As Orient bent there her breath stirred the dark lock of hair on the brow, and the slight and airy motion of itself brought into forceful being all the awful immobility and silence of death.

"He does not breathe! His heart does not beat! Will he never open his eyes again?" she said. "O Reymund, Reymund, I love you!"

She bent nearer as she sighed the words, and her lips were sealed to his.

A quiver ran through all the frozen frame reposing there beside her, a pulse of warmth, perhaps, played in the hand hers clasped; the eyelids shook and lifted and unveiled the dark and woful eyes.

"You have seen my soul, Orient," said Reymund. "Good by."

The dark and woful eyes were veiled again. And this time Reymund's soul was gone beyond recall.

THE FALL OF THE HOUSE OF USHER
BY EDGAR ALLAN POE.

Son cœur est un luth suspendu;
Sitôt qu'on le touche il rèsonne.
DE BERANGER.

DURING the whole of a dull, dark, and soundless day in the autumn of the year, when the clouds hung oppressively low in the heavens, I had been passing alone, on horseback, through a singularly dreary tract of country; and at length found myself, as the shades of the evening drew on, within view of the melancholy House of Usher. I know not how it was, but, with the first glimpse of the building, a sense of insufferable gloom pervaded my spirit. I say insufferable; for the feeling was unrelieved by any of that half-pleasurable, because poetic, sentiment, with which the mind usually receives even the sternest natural images of the desolate or terrible. I looked upon the scene before me,—upon the mere house and the simple landscape features of the domain,—upon the bleak walls,—upon the vacant, eye-like windows,—upon a few rank sedges,—and upon a few white trunks of decayed trees,—with an utter depression of soul which I can compare to no earthly sensation more properly than to the after-dream of the reveller upon opium,—the bitter lapse into every-day life,—the hideous dropping off of the veil. There was an iciness, a sinking, a sickening of the heart,—an unredeemed dreariness of thought which no goading of the imagination could torture into aught of the sublime. What was it,—I paused to think,—what was it that so unnerved me in the contemplation of the House of Usher? It was a mystery all insoluble; nor could I grapple with the shadowy fancies that crowded upon me as I pondered. I was forced to fall back upon the unsatisfactory conclusion that, while, beyond doubt, there *are* combinations of very simple natural objects which have the power of thus affecting us, still the analysis of this power lies among considerations beyond our depth. It was possible, I reflected, that a mere different arrangement of the particulars of the scene, of the details of the picture, would be sufficient to modify, or perhaps to annihilate, its capacity for sorrowful impression; and, acting upon this idea, I reined my horse to the precipitous brink of a black and lurid tarn that lay in unruffled lustre by the dwelling, and gazed down—but with a shudder even more thrilling than before—upon the remodelled and inverted images of the gray sedge and the ghastly tree-stems and the vacant and eye-like windows.

Nevertheless, in this mansion of gloom I now proposed to myself a sojourn of some weeks. Its proprietor, Roderick Usher, had been one of my boon companions in boyhood; but many years had elapsed since our last meeting. A letter, however, had lately reached me in a distant part of the country,—a letter from him,—which, in its wildly importunate nature, had admitted of no other than a personal reply. The manuscript gave evidence of nervous agitation. The writer spoke of acute bodily illness,—of a mental disorder which oppressed him,—and of an earnest desire to see me, as his best, and indeed his only personal friend, with a view of attempting, by the cheerfulness of my society, some alleviation of his malady. It was the manner in which all this, and much more, was said,—it was the apparent *heart* that went with his request,—which allowed me no room for hesitation; and I accordingly obeyed forthwith what I still considered a very singular summons.

Although as boys we had been even intimate associates, yet I really knew little of my friend. His reserve had been always excessive and habitual. I was aware, however, that his very ancient family had been noted, time out of mind, for a peculiar sensibility of temperament, displaying itself, through long ages, in many works of exalted art, and manifested, of late, in repeated deeds of munificent yet unobtrusive charity, as well as in a passionate devotion to the intricacies, perhaps even more than to the orthodox and easily recognizable beauties, of musical science. I had learned, too, the very remarkable fact that the stem of the Usher race, all time-honored as it was, had put forth, at no period, any enduring branch; in other words, that the entire family lay in the direct line of descent, and had always, with very trifling and very temporary variation, so lain. It was this deficiency, I considered, while running over in thought the perfect keeping of the character of the premises with the accredited character of the people, and while speculating upon the possible influence which the one, in the long lapse of centuries, might have exercised upon the other,—it was this deficiency, perhaps, of collateral issue, and the consequent undeviating transmission, from sire to son, of the patrimony with the name, which had, at length, so identified the two as to merge the original title of the estate in the quaint and equivocal appellation of the "House of Usher,"—an appellation which seemed to include, in the minds of the peasantry who used it, both the family and the family mansion.

I have said that the sole effect of my somewhat childish experiment—that of looking down within the tarn—had been to deepen the first singular impression. There can be no doubt that the consciousness of the rapid increase of my superstition—for why should I not so term it?—served mainly to accelerate the increase itself. Such, I have long known, is the paradoxical law of all sentiments having terror as a basis. And it might have been for this reason only that, when I again uplifted my eyes to the house itself, from its image in the pool, there grew in my mind a strange fancy,—a fancy so ridiculous, indeed, that I but mention it to show the vivid force of the sensations which oppressed me. I had so worked upon my imagination as really to believe that about the whole mansion and domain hung an atmosphere peculiar to themselves and their immediate vicinity,—an atmosphere which had no affinity with the air of heaven, but which had reeked up from the decayed trees and the gray wall and the silent tarn,—a pestilent and mystic vapor, dull, sluggish, faintly discernible, and leaden-hued.

Shaking off from my spirit what *must* have been a dream, I scanned more narrowly the real aspect of the building. Its principal feature seemed to be that of an excessive antiquity. The discoloration of ages had been great. Minute fungi overspread the whole exterior, hanging in a fine, tangled web-work from the eaves. Yet all this was apart from any extraordinary dilapidation. No portion of the masonry had fallen; and there appeared to be a wild inconsistency between its still perfect adaptation of parts and the crumbling condition of the individual stones. In this there was much that reminded me of the specious totality of old woodwork which has rotted for long years in some neglected vault, with no disturbance from the breath of the external air. Beyond this indication of extensive decay, however, the fabric gave little token of instability. Perhaps the eye of a scrutinizing observer might have discovered a barely perceptible fissure, which, extending from the roof of the building in front, made its way down the wall in a zigzag direction, until it became lost in the sullen waters of the tarn.

Noticing these things, I rode over a short causeway to the house. A servant in waiting took my horse, and I entered the Gothic archway of the hall. A valet, of stealthy step, thence conducted me, in silence, through many dark and intricate passages in my progress to the studio of his master. Much that I encountered on the way contributed, I know not how, to heighten the vague sentiments of which I have already spoken. While the objects around me,—while the carvings of the ceilings, the sombre tapestries of the walls, the ebon blackness of the floors, and the phantasmagoric armorial trophies which rattled as I strode, were but matters to which, or to such as which, I had been accustomed from my infancy,—while I hesitated not to acknowledge how familiar was all this, I still wondered to find how unfamiliar were the fancies which ordinary images were stirring up. On one of the staircases, I met the physician of the family. His countenance, I thought, wore a mingled expression of low cunning and perplexity. He accosted me with trepidation, and passed on. The valet now threw open a door and ushered me into the presence of his master.

The room in which I found myself was very large and lofty. The windows were long, narrow, and pointed, and at so vast a distance from the black oaken floor as to be altogether inaccessible from within. Feeble gleams of encrimsoned light made their way through the trellised panes, and served to render sufficiently distinct the more prominent objects around; the eye, however, struggled in vain to reach the remoter angles of the chamber, or the recesses of the vaulted and fretted ceiling. Dark draperies hung upon the walls. The general furniture was profuse, comfortless, antique, and tattered. Many books and musical instruments lay scattered about, but failed to give any vitality to the scene. I felt that I breathed an atmosphere of sorrow. An air of stern, deep, and irredeemable gloom hung over and pervaded all.

Upon my entrance, Usher arose from a sofa on which he had been lying at full length, and greeted me with a vivacious warmth which had much in it, I at first thought, of an overdone cordiality,—of the constrained effort of the *ennuyé* man of the world. A glance, however, at his countenance, convinced me of his perfect sincerity. We sat down; and for some moments, while he spoke not, I gazed upon him with a feeling half of pity, half of awe. Surely, man had never before so terribly altered, in so brief a period, as had Roderick Usher! It was with difficulty that I could bring myself to admit the identity of the wan being before me with the companion of my early boyhood. Yet the character of his face had been at all times remarkable. A cadaverousness of complexion; an eye large, liquid, and luminous beyond comparison; lips somewhat thin and very pallid, but of a surpassingly beautiful curve; a nose of a delicate Hebrew model, but with a breadth of nostril unusual in similar formations; a finely moulded chin, speaking, in its want of prominence, of a want of moral energy; hair of a more than web-like softness and tenuity;—these features, with an inordinate expansion above the regions of the temple, made up altogether a countenance not easily to be forgotten. And now in the mere exaggeration of the prevailing character of these features, and of the expression they were wont to convey, lay so much of change that I doubted to whom I spoke. The now ghastly pallor of the skin, and the now miraculous lustre of the eye, above all things startled and even awed me. The silken hair, too, had been suffered to grow all unheeded, and as, in its wild gossamer texture, it floated rather than fell about the face, I could not, even with effort, connect its Arabesque expression with any idea of simple humanity.

In the manner of my friend I was at once struck with an incoherence,—an inconsistency; and I soon found this to arise from a series of feeble and futile struggles to overcome an habitual trepidancy,—an excessive nervous agitation. For something of this nature I had indeed been prepared, no less by his letter than by reminiscences of certain boyish traits, and by conclusions deduced from his peculiar physical conformation and temperament. His action was alternately vivacious and sullen. His voice varied rapidly from a tremulous indecision (when the animal spirits seemed utterly in abeyance) to that species of energetic concision,—that abrupt, weighty, unhurried, and hollow-sounding enunciation,—that leaden, self-balanced, and perfectly modulated guttural utterance, which may be observed in the lost drunkard, or the irreclaimable eater of opium, during the periods of his most intense excitement.

It was thus that he spoke of the object of my visit, of his earnest desire to see me, and of the solace he expected me to afford him. He entered, at some length, into what he conceived to be the nature of his malady. It was, he said, a constitutional and a family evil, and one for which he despaired to find a remedy,—a mere nervous affection, he immediately added, which would undoubtedly soon pass off. It displayed itself in a host of unnatural sensations. Some of these, as he detailed them, interested and bewildered me; although, perhaps, the terms, and the general manner of the narration had their weight. He suffered much from a morbid acuteness of the senses; the most insipid food was alone endurable; he could wear only garments of certain texture; the odors of all flowers were oppressive; his eyes were tortured by even a faint light; and there were but peculiar sounds, and these from stringed instruments, which did not inspire him with horror.

To an anomalous species of terror I found him a bounden slave. "I shall perish," said he, "I *must* perish in this deplorable folly. Thus, thus, and not otherwise, shall I be lost. I dread the events of the future, not in themselves, but in their results. I shudder at the thought of any, even the most trivial, incident, which may operate upon this intolerable agitation of soul. I have, indeed, no abhorrence of danger, except in its absolute effect,—in terror. In this unnerved, in this pitiable condition, I feel that the period will sooner or later arrive when I must abandon life and reason together, in some struggle with the grim phantasm, FEAR."

I learned, moreover, at intervals, and through broken and equivocal hints, another singular feature of his mental condition. He was enchained by certain superstitious impressions in regard to the dwelling which he tenanted, and whence, for many years, he had never ventured forth,—in regard to an influence whose supposititious force was conveyed in terms too shadowy here to be restated,—an influence which some peculiarities in the mere form and substance of his family mansion had, by dint of long sufferance, he said, obtained over his spirit,—an effect which the *physique* of the gray walls and turrets, and of the dim tarn into which they all looked down, had at length brought about upon the *morale* of his existence.

He admitted, however, although with hesitation, that much of the peculiar gloom which thus afflicted him could be traced to a more natural and far more palpable origin,—to the severe and long-continued illness—indeed to the evidently approaching dissolution—of a tenderly beloved sister,—his sole companion for long years,—his last and only relative on earth. "Her decease," he said with a bitterness which I can never forget, "would leave him (him the hopeless and the frail) the last of the ancient race of the Ushers." While he spoke, the lady Madeline (for so was she called) passed slowly through a remote portion of the apartment, and, without having noticed my presence, disappeared. I regarded her with an utter astonishment, not unmingled with dread,—and yet I found it impossible to account for such feelings. A sensation of stupor oppressed me, as my eyes followed her retreating steps. When a door, at length, closed upon her, my glance sought instinctively and eagerly the countenance of the brother; but he had buried his face in his hands, and I could only perceive that a far more than ordinary wanness had overspread the emaciated fingers through which trickled many passionate tears.

The disease of the lady Madeline had long baffled the skill of her physicians. A settled apathy, a gradual wasting away of the person, and frequent although transient affections of a partially cataleptical character, were the unusual diagnosis. Hitherto she had steadily borne up against the pressure of her malady, and had not betaken herself finally to bed; but, on the closing in of the evening of my arrival at the house, she succumbed (as her brother told me at night with inexpressible agitation) to the prostrating power of the destroyer; and I learned that the glimpse I had obtained of her person would thus probably be the last I should obtain,—that the lady, at least while living, would be seen by me no more.

For several days ensuing, her name was unmentioned by either Usher or myself; and during this period I was busied in earnest endeavors to alleviate the melancholy of my friend. We painted and read together; or I listened, as if in a dream, to the wild improvisations of his speaking guitar. And thus, as a closer and still closer intimacy admitted me more unreservedly into the recesses of his spirit, the more bitterly did I perceive the futility of all attempt at cheering a mind from which darkness, as if an inherent, positive quality, poured forth upon all objects of the moral and physical universe, in one unceasing radiation of gloom.

I shall ever bear about me a memory of the many solemn hours I thus spent alone with the master of the House of Usher. Yet I should fail in any attempt to convey an idea of the exact character of the studies, or of the occupations, in which he involved me, or led me the way. An excited and highly distempered ideality threw a sulphureous lustre over all. His long, improvised dirges will ring forever in my ears. Among other things, I hold painfully in mind a certain singular perversion and amplification of the wild air of the last waltz of Von Weber. From the paintings over which his elaborate fancy brooded, and which grew, touch by touch, into vaguenesses at which I shuddered the more thrillingly, because I shuddered knowing not why,—from these paintings (vivid as their images now are before me) I would in vain endeavor to educe more than a small portion which should lie within the compass of merely written words. By the utter simplicity, by the nakedness of his designs, he arrested and overawed attention. If ever mortal painted an idea, that mortal was Roderick Usher. For me at least—in the circumstances then surrounding me—arose, out of the pure abstractions which the hypochondriac contrived to throw upon his canvas, an intensity of intolerable awe, no shadow of which felt I ever yet in the contemplation of the certainly glowing yet too concrete reveries of Fuseli.

One of the phantasmagoric conceptions of my friend, partaking not so rigidly of the spirit of abstraction, may be shadowed forth, although feebly, in words. A small picture presented the interior of an immensely long and rectangular vault or tunnel, with low walls, smooth, white, and without interruption or device. Certain accessory points of the design served well to convey the idea that this excavation lay at an exceeding depth below the surface of the earth. No outlet was observed in any portion of its vast extent, and no torch, or other artificial source of light was discernible; yet a flood of intense rays rolled throughout, and bathed the whole in a ghastly and inappropriate splendor.

I have just spoken of that morbid condition of the auditory nerve which rendered all music intolerable to the sufferer, with the exception of certain effects of stringed instruments. It was, perhaps, the narrow limits to which he thus confined himself upon the guitar, which gave birth, in great measure, to the fantastic character of his performances. But the fervid facility of his impromptus could not be so accounted for. They must have been, and were, in the notes, as well as in the words of his wild fantasias (for he not unfrequently accompanied himself with rhymed verbal improvisations), the result of that intense mental collectedness and concentration to which I have previously alluded as observable only in particular moments of the highest artificial excitement. The words of one of these rhapsodies I have easily remembered. I was, perhaps, the more forcibly impressed with it as he gave it, because, in the under or mystic current of its meaning, I fancied that I perceived, and for the first time, a full consciousness, on the part of Usher, of the tottering of his lofty reason upon her throne. The verses, which were entitled "The Haunted Palace," ran very nearly, if not accurately, thus:—

In the greenest of our valleys,
By good angels tenanted,
Once a fair and stately palace palace—
Radiant palace—reared its head.
In the monarch Thought's dominion,—
It stood there!
Never seraph spread a pinion
Over fabric half so fair.

Banners yellow, glorious, golden,
On its roof did float and flow
(This—all this—was in the olden
Time long ago);
And every gentle air that dallied,
In that sweet day,
Along the ramparts plumed and pallid,
A winged odor went away.

Wanderers in that happy valley
Through two luminous windows saw
Spirits moving musically
To a lute's well-tunéd law,
Round about a throne, where sitting
(Porphyrogene!)
In state his glory well befitting,
The ruler of the realm was seen.

And all with pearl and ruby glowing
Was the fair palace door,
Through which came flowing, flowing, flowing
And sparkling evermore,
A troop of Echoes whose sweet duty
Was but to sing,
In voices of surpassing beauty,
The wit and wisdom of their king.

But evil things, in robes of sorrow,
Assailed the monarch's high estate;
(Ah, let us mourn, for never morrow
Shall dawn upon him, desolate!)
And, round about his home, the glory
That blushed and bloomed

Is but a dim-remembered story
Of the old time entombed.

And travellers now within that valley,
Through the red-litten windows, see
Vast forms that move fantastically
To a discordant melody;
While, like a rapid, ghastly river,
Through the pale door,
A hideous throng rush out forever,
And laugh,—but smile no more.

I well remember that suggestions arising from this ballad led us into a train of thought wherein became manifest an opinion of Usher's which I mention not so much on account of its novelty (for other men have thought thus) as on account of the pertinacity with which he maintained it. This opinion, in its general form, was that of the sentience of all vegetable things. But, in his disordered fancy, the idea had assumed a more daring character, and trespassed, under certain conditions, upon the kingdom of inorganization. I lack words to express the full extent or the earnest *abandon* of his persuasion. The belief, however, was connected (as I have previously hinted) with the gray stones of the home of his forefathers. The conditions of the sentience had been here, he imagined, fulfilled in the method of collocation of these stones,—in the order of their arrangement, as well as in that of the many *fungi* which overspread them, and of the decayed trees which stood around,—above all, in the long undisturbed endurance of this arrangement, and in its reduplication in the still waters of the tarn. Its evidence—the evidence of the sentience—was to be seen, he said (and I here started as he spoke) in the gradual yet certain condensation of an atmosphere of their own about the waters and the walls. The result was discoverable, he added, in that silent, yet importunate and terrible influence which for centuries had moulded the destinies of his family, and which made *him* what I now saw him,—what he was. Such opinions need no comment, and I will make none.

Our books—the books which, for years, had formed no small portion of the mental existence of the invalid—were, as might be supposed, in strict keeping with this character of phantasm. We pored together over such works as the Ververt et Chartreuse of Gresset; the Belphegor of Machiavelli; the Heaven and Hell of Swedenborg; the Subterranean Voyage of Nicholas Klimm by Holberg; the Chiromancy of Robert Flud, of Jean d'Indaginé, and of De la Chambre; the Journey into the Blue Distance of Tieck; and the City of the Sun of Campanella. One favorite volume was a small octavo edition of the *Directorium Inquisitorium*, by the Dominican Eymeric de Gironne; and there were passages in Pomponius Mela, about the old African Satyrs and Œgipans, over which Usher would sit dreaming for hours. His chief delight, however, was found in the perusal of an exceedingly rare and curious book in quarto Gothic,—the manual of a forgotten church,—the *Vigiliæ Mortuorum secundum Chorum Ecclesiæ Maguntinæ*.

I could not help thinking of the wild ritual of this work, and of its probable influence upon the hypochondriac, when, one evening, having informed me abruptly that the lady Madeline was no more, he stated his intention of preserving her corpse for a fortnight (previously to its final interment) in one of the numerous vaults within the main walls of the building. The worldly reason, however, assigned for this singular proceeding, was one which I did not feel at liberty to dispute. The brother had been led to his resolution (so he told me) by consideration of the unusual character of the malady of the deceased, of certain obtrusive and eager inquiries on the part of her medical men, and of the remote and exposed situation of the burial-ground of the family. I will not deny that when I called to mind the sinister countenance of the person whom I met upon the staircase, on the day of my arrival at the house, I had no desire to oppose what I regarded as at best but a harmless, and by no means an unnatural precaution.

At the request of Usher, I personally aided him in the arrangements for the temporary entombment. The body having been encoffined, we two alone bore it to its rest. The vault in which we placed it (and which had been so long unopened that our torches, half smothered in its oppressive atmosphere, gave us little opportunity for investigation) was small, damp, and entirely without means of admission for light; lying, at great depth, immediately beneath that portion of the building in which was my own sleeping-apartment. It had been used, apparently, in remote feudal times, for the worst purposes of a donjon-keep, and, in later days, as a place of deposit for powder, or some other highly combustible substance, as a portion of its floor, and the whole interior of a long archway through which we reached it, were carefully sheathed with copper. The door of massive iron had been, also, similarly protected. Its immense weight caused an unusually sharp, grating sound, as it moved upon its hinges.

Having deposited our mournful burden upon tressels within this region of horror, we partially turned aside the yet unscrewed lid of the coffin, and looked upon the face of the tenant. A striking similitude between the brother and sister now first arrested my attention; and Usher, divining, perhaps, my thoughts, murmured out some few words from which I learned that the deceased and himself had been twins, and that sympathies of a scarcely intelligible nature had always existed between them. Our glances, however, rested not long upon the dead,—for we could not regard her unawed. The disease which had thus entombed the lady in the maturity of youth, had left, as usual in all maladies of a strictly cataleptical character, the mockery of a faint blush upon the bosom and the face, and that suspiciously lingering smile upon the lip which is so terrible in death. We replaced and screwed down the lid, and, having secured the door of iron, made our way, with toil, into the scarcely less gloomy apartments of the upper portion of the house.

And now, some days of bitter grief having elapsed, an observable change came over the features of the mental disorder of my friend. His ordinary manner had vanished. His ordinary occupations were neglected or forgotten. He roamed from chamber to chamber with hurried, unequal, and objectless step. The pallor of his countenance had assumed, if possible, a more ghastly hue,—but the luminousness of his eye had utterly gone out. The once occasional huskiness of his tone was heard no more; and a tremulous quaver, as if of extreme terror, habitually characterized his utterance. There were times, indeed, when I thought his unceasingly agitated mind was laboring with some oppressive secret, to divulge which he struggled for the necessary courage. At times, again, I was obliged to resolve all into the mere inexplicable vagaries of madness, for I beheld him gazing upon vacancy for long hours, in an attitude of the profoundest attention, as if listening to some imaginary sound. It was no wonder that his condition terrified, that it infected me. I felt creeping upon me, by slow yet certain degrees, the wild influences of his own fantastic yet impressive superstitions.

It was, especially, upon retiring to bed late in the night of the seventh or eighth day after the placing of the lady Madeline within the donjon, that I experienced the full power of such feelings. Sleep came not near my couch,—while the hours waned and waned away. I struggled to reason off the nervousness which had dominion over me. I endeavored to believe that much, if not all, of what I felt was due to the bewildering influence of the gloomy furniture of the room,—of the dark and tattered draperies, which, tortured into motion by the breath of a rising tempest, swayed fitfully to and fro upon the walls, and rustled uneasily about the decorations of the bed. But my efforts were fruitless. An irrepressible tremor gradually pervaded my frame; and, at length, upon my very heart sat an incubus of utterly causeless alarm. Shaking this off with a gasp and a struggle, I uplifted myself on the pillows, and, peering earnestly within the intense darkness of the chamber, hearkened—I know not why, except that an instinctive spirit prompted me—to certain low and indefinite sounds which came, through the pauses of the storm, at long intervals, I knew not whence. Overpowered by an intense sentiment of horror, unaccountable yet unendurable, I threw on my clothes with haste (for I felt that I should sleep no more during the night), and endeavored to arouse myself from the pitiable condition into which I had fallen, by pacing rapidly to and fro through the apartment.

I had taken but few turns in this manner, when a light step on an adjoining staircase arrested my attention. I presently recognized it as that of Usher. In an instant afterward he rapped, with a gentle touch, at my door, and entered, bearing a lamp. His countenance was, as usual, cadaverously wan; but, moreover, there was a species of mad hilarity in his eyes,—an evidently restrained *hysteria* in his whole demeanor. His air appalled me; but anything was preferable to the solitude which I had so long endured, and I even welcomed his presence as a relief.

"And you have not seen it?" he said abruptly, after having stared about him for some moments in silence,—"you have not then seen it?—but, stay! you shall." Thus speaking, and having carefully shaded his lamp, he hurried to one of the casements, and threw it freely open to the storm.

The impetuous fury of the entering gust nearly lifted us from our feet. It was, indeed, a tempestuous yet sternly beautiful night, and one wildly singular in its terror and its beauty. A whirlwind had apparently collected its force in our vicinity; for there were frequent and violent alterations in the direction of the wind; and the exceeding density of the clouds (which hung so low as to press upon the turrets of the house) did not prevent our perceiving the life-like velocity with which they flew careering from all points against each other, without passing away into the distance. I say that even their exceeding density did not prevent our perceiving this; yet we had no glimpse of the moon or stars, nor was there any flashing forth of the lightning. But the under surfaces of the huge masses of agitated vapor, as well as all terrestrial objects immediately around us, were glowing in the unnatural light of a faintly luminous and distinctly visible gaseous exhalation which hung about and enshrouded the mansion.

"You must not, you shall not behold this!" said I, shudderingly, to Usher, as I led him, with a gentle violence, from the window to a seat. "These appearances, which bewilder you, are merely electrical phenomena not uncommon; or it may be that they have their ghastly origin in the rank miasma of the tarn. Let us close this casement; the air is chilling and dangerous to your frame. Here is one of your favorite romances. I will read, and you shall listen; and so we will pass away this terrible night together."

The antique volume which I had taken up was the Mad Trist of Sir Launcelot Canning; but I had called it a favorite of Usher's more in sad jest than in earnest; for, in truth, there is little in its uncouth and unimaginative prolixity which could have had interest for the lofty and spiritual ideality of my friend. It was, however, the only book immediately at hand; and I indulged a vague hope that the excitement which now agitated the hypochondriac might find relief (for the history of mental disorder is full of similar anomalies) even in the extremeness of the folly which I should read. Could I have judged, indeed, by the wild, overstrained air of vivacity with which he hearkened, or apparently hearkened, to the words of the tale, I might well have congratulated myself upon the success of my design.

I had arrived at that well-known portion of the story where Ethelred, the hero of the Trist, having sought in vain for peaceable admission into the dwelling of the hermit, proceeds to make good an entrance by force. Here, it will be remembered, the words of the narrative run thus:—

"And Ethelred, who was by nature of a doughty heart, and who was now mighty withal, on account of the powerfulness of the wine which he had drunken, waited no longer to hold parley with the hermit, who, in sooth, was of an obstinate and maliceful turn, but, feeling the rain upon his shoulders, and fearing the rising of the tempest, uplifted his mace outright, and, with blows, made quickly room in the plankings of the door for his gauntleted hand; and now pulling therewith sturdily, he so cracked, and ripped, and tore all asunder, that the noise of the dry and hollow-sounding wood alarumed and reverberated throughout the forest."

At the termination of this sentence I started, and for a moment paused; for it appeared to me (although I at once concluded that my excited fancy had deceived me),—it appeared to me that, from some very remote portion of the mansion, came indistinctly to my ears what might have been, in its exact similarity of character, the echo (but a stifled and dull one certainly) of the very cracking and ripping sound which Sir Launcelot had so particularly described. It was, beyond doubt, the coincidence alone which had arrested my attention; for, amid the rattling of the sashes of the casements, and the ordinary commingled noises of the still increasing storm, the sound, in itself, had nothing, surely, which should have interested or disturbed me. I continued the story.

"But the good champion Ethelred, now entering within the door, was sore enraged and amazed to perceive no signal of the maliceful hermit; but, in the stead thereof, a dragon of a scaly and prodigious demeanor, and of a fiery tongue, which sate in guard before a palace of gold, with a floor of silver; and upon the wall there hung a shield of shining brass with this legend enwritten:—

'Who entereth herein, a conqueror hath bin;
Who slayeth the dragon, the shield he shall win.'

And Ethelred uplifted his mace, and struck upon the head of the dragon, which fell before him, and gave up his pesty breath, with a shriek so horrid and harsh, and withal so piercing, that Ethelred had fain to close his ears with his hands against the dreadful noise of it, the like whereof was never before heard."

Here again I paused abruptly, and now with a feeling of wild amazement; for there could be no doubt whatever that, in this instance, I did actually hear (although from what direction it proceeded I found it impossible to say) a low and apparently distant, but harsh, protracted, and most unusual screaming or grating sound,—the exact counterpart of what my fancy had already conjured up for the dragon's unnatural shriek as described by the romancer.

Oppressed, as I certainly was, upon the occurrence of this second and most extraordinary coincidence, by a thousand conflicting sensations, in which wonder and extreme terror were predominant, I still retained sufficient presence of mind to avoid exciting, by any observation, the sensitive nervousness of my companion. I was by no means certain that he had noticed the sounds in question; although, assuredly, a strange alteration had, during the last few minutes, taken place in his demeanor. From a position fronting my own, he had gradually brought round his chair, so as to sit with his face to the door of the chamber; and thus I could but partially perceive his features, although I saw that his lips trembled as if he were murmuring inaudibly. His head had dropped upon his breast; yet I knew that he was not asleep, from the wide and rigid opening of the eye as I caught a glance of it in profile. The motion of his body, too, was at variance with this idea; for he rocked from side to side with a gentle yet constant and uniform sway. Having rapidly taken notice of all this, I resumed the narrative of Sir Launcelot, which thus proceeded:—

"And now the champion, having escaped from the terrible fury of the dragon, bethinking himself of the brazen shield, and of the breaking up of the enchantment which was upon it, removed the carcass from out of the way before him, and approached valorously over the silver pavement of the castle to where the shield was upon the wall; which in sooth tarried not for his full coming, but fell down at his feet upon the silver floor, with a mighty great and terrible ringing sound."

No sooner had these syllables passed my lips, than—as if a shield of brass had indeed, at the moment, fallen heavily upon a floor of silver—I became aware of a distinct, hollow, metallic, and clangorous, yet apparently muffled reverberation. Completely unnerved, I leaped to my feet; but the measured rocking movement of Usher was undisturbed. I rushed to the chair in which he sat. His eyes were bent fixedly before him, and throughout his whole countenance reigned a stony rigidity. But, as I placed my hand upon his shoulder, there came a strong shudder over his whole person; a sickly smile quivered about his lips; and I saw that he spoke in a low, hurried, and gibbering murmur, as if unconscious of my presence. Bending closely over him, I at length drank in the hideous import of his words.

"Not hear it?—yes, I hear it, and *have* heard it. Long—long—long—many minutes, many hours, many days, have I heard it—yet I dared not—O, pity me, miserable wretch that I am!—I dared not—I *dared* not speak! *We have put her living in the tomb!* Said I not that my senses were acute? I *now* tell you that I heard her first feeble movements in the hollow coffin. I heard them—many, many days ago—yet I dared not—*I dared not speak!* And now—to-night—Ethelred—ha! ha!—the breaking of the hermit's door, and the death-cry of the dragon, and the clangor of the shield!—say, rather, the rending of her coffin, and the grating of the iron hinges of her prison, and her struggles within the coppered archway of the vault! O, whither shall I fly? Will she not be here anon? Is she not hurrying to upbraid me for my haste? Have I not heard her footstep on the stair? Do I not distinguish that heavy and horrible beating of her heart? Madman!"—here he sprang furiously to his feet, and shrieked out his syllables, as if in the effort he were giving up his soul,—"*Madman! I tell you that she now stands without the door!*"

As if in the superhuman energy of his utterance had been found the potency of a spell, the huge antique panels to which the speaker pointed threw slowly back, upon the instant, their ponderous and ebony jaws. It was the work of the rushing gust; but then without those doors *did* stand the lofty and enshrouded figure of the lady Madeline of Usher. There was blood upon her white robes, and the evidence of some bitter struggle upon every portion of her emaciated frame. For a moment she remained trembling and reeling to and fro upon the threshold, then, with a low moaning cry, fell heavily inward upon the person of her brother, and in her violent and now final death-agonies bore him to the floor a corpse, and a victim to the terrors he had anticipated.From that chamber, and from that mansion, I fled aghast. The storm was still abroad in all its wrath as I found myself crossing the old causeway. Suddenly there shot along the path a wild light, and I turned to see whence a gleam so unusual could have issued; for the vast house and its shadows were alone behind me. The radiance was that of the full, setting, and blood-red moon, which now shone vividly through that once barely discernible fissure, of which I have before spoken as extending from the roof of the building, in a zigzag direction, to the base. While I gazed, this fissure rapidly widened,—there came a fierce breath of the whirlwind,—the entire orb of the satellite burst at once upon my sight,—my brain reeled as I saw the mighty walls rushing asunder,—there was a long, tumultuous, shouting sound like the voice of a thousand waters,—and the deep and dank tarn at my feet closed sullenly and silently over the fragments of the House of Usher.

CHOPS THE DWARF.
BY CHARLES DICKENS.

A one period of its reverses, the House to Let fell into the hands of a showman. He was found registered as its occupier, on the parish books of the time when he rented the House, and there was therefore no need of any clew to his name. But he himself was less easy to be found; for he had led a wandering life, and settled people had lost sight of him, and people who plumed themselves on being respectable were shy of admitting that they had ever known anything of him. At last among the marsh lands near the river's level, that lie about Deptford and the neighboring market-gardens, a grizzled personage in velveteen, with a face so cut up by varieties of weather that he looked as if he had been tattooed, was found smoking a pipe at the door of a wooden house on wheels. The wooden house was laid up in ordinary for the winter near the mouth of a muddy creek; and everything near it—the foggy river, the misty marshes, and the steaming market-gardens—smoked in company with the grizzled man. In the midst of the smoking party, the funnel-chimney of the wooden house on wheels was not remiss, but took its pipe with the rest in a companionable manner.

On being asked if it were he who had once rented the House to Let, Grizzled Velveteen looked surprised, and said yes. Then his name was Magsman. That was it, Toby Magsman,—which was lawfully christened Robert; but called in the line, from an infant, Toby. There was nothing agin Toby Magsman, he believed? If there was suspicion of such, mention it!

There was no suspicion of such, he might rest assured. But some inquiries were making about that house, and would he object to say why he left it?

Not at all; why should he? He left it along of a dwarf.

Along of a dwarf?

Mr. Magsman repeated, deliberately and emphatically, "Along of a dwarf."

Might it be compatible with Mr. Magsman's inclination and convenience to enter, as a favor, into a few particulars?

Mr. Magsman entered into the following particulars:—

It was a long time ago to begin with,—afore lotteries and a deal more was done away with. Mr. Magsman was looking around for a good pitch, and he see that house, and he says to himself, "I'll have you if you are to be had. If money'll get you, I'll have you."

The neighbors cut up rough, and made complaints; but Mr. Magsman don't know what they all would have had. It was a lovely thing. First of all, there was the canvas representin the pictur of the Giant in Spanish trunks and a ruff, who was half the height of the house, and was run up with a line and pulley to a pole of the roof, so that his Ed was coeval with the parapet. Then there was the canvas representin the pictur of the Albina lady, showin her white 'air to the Army and Navy in correct uniform. Then there was the canvas representin the pictur of the Wild Indian scalpin a member of some foreign nation. Then there was the canvas representin the pictur of a child of a British planter seized by two Boa-Constrictors,—not that we never had no child, nor no Constrictors neither. Similarly, there was the canvas representin the pictur of the Wild Ass of the Prairies,—not that we never had no wild asses, nor wouldn't have had 'em as a gift. Last there was the canvas representin the pictur of the Dwarf, and like him too (considerin), with George the Fourth in such a state of astonishment at him as his Majesty couldn't with his utmost politeness and stoutness express. The front of the House was so covered with canvases that there wasn't a spark of daylight ever visible on that side. "MAGSMAN'S AMUSEMENTS," fifteen foot long by two foot high, ran over the front door and parlor winders. The passage was a arbor of green baize and garden stuff. A barrel-organ performed there unceasing. And as to respectability,—if threepence ain't respectable, what is?

But the Dwarf is the principal article at present, and he was worth money. He was wrote up as "Major Tpschoffki, of the Imperial Bulgraderian Brigade." Nobody couldn't pronounce the name, and it never was intended anybody should. The public always turned it, as a regular rule, into Chopski. In the line he was called Chops; partly on that account, and partly because his real name, if he ever had any real name (which was very dubious), was Stakes.

He was an uncommon small man, he really was. Certainly not so small as he was made out to be, but where's your dwarf as is? He was a most uncommon small man, with a most uncommon large Ed; and what he had inside that Ed nobody never knowed but himself; even supposin himself to have ever took stock of it, which it would have been a stiff job for him to do. The kindest little man as never growed!—spirited, but not proud. When he travelled with the Spotted Baby, though he knowed himself to be a nat'ral Dwarf, and knowed the Baby's spots to be put onto him artificial, he nursed that Baby like a mother. You never heard him give a ill name to a giant. He did allow himself to break out into strong language respectin the Fat Lady from Norfolk; but that was an affair of the 'art; and when a man's 'art has been trifled with by a lady, and the preference giv to a Indian, he ain't master of his actions.

He was always in love, of course; every human nat'ral phenomenon is. And he was always in love with a large woman; I never knowed the dwarf as could be got to love a small one. Which helps to keep 'em the curiosities they are.

One sing'lar idea he had in that Ed of his, which must have meant something, or it wouldn't have been there. It was always his opinion that he was entitled to property. He never put his name to anything. He had been taught to write by a young man without any arms, who got his living with his toes (quite a writing-master *he* was, and taught scores in the line), but Chops would have starved to death afore he'd gained a bit of bread by putting his hand to a paper. This is the more curious to bear in mind, because HE had no property, except his house and a sarser. When I say his house, I mean the box, painted and got up outside like a reg'ler six-roomer, that he used to creep into, with a diamond ring (or quite as good to look at) on his forefinger, and ring a little bell out of what the public believed to be the drawing-room winder. And when I say a sarser, I mean a Cheney sarser in which he made a collection for himself at the end of every entertainment. His cue for that he took from me: "Ladies and gentlemen, the little man will now walk three times round the Cairawan, and retire behind the curtain." When he said anything important, in private life, he mostly wound it up with this form of words, and they was generally the last thing he said to me afore he went to bed.

He had what I consider a fine mind,—a poetic mind. His ideas respectin his property never come upon him so strong as when he sat upon a barrel-organ and had the handle turned. Arter the wibration had run through him a little time, he would screech out: "Toby, I feel my property coming,—grind away! I'm counting my guineas by thousands, Toby,—grind away! Toby, I shall be a man of fortun! I feel the mint a jingling in me, Toby, and I'm swelling out into the Bank of England!" Such is the influence of music on the poetic mind. Not that he was partial to any other music but a barrel-organ; on the contrairy, he hated it.

He had a kind of everlasting grudge agin the public; which is a thing you may notice in many phenomenons that get their living out of it. What riled him most in the nater of his occupation was that it kep him out of society. He was continiwally sayin: "Toby, my ambition is to go into society. The curse of my position towards the public is that it keeps me hout of society. This don't signify to a low beast of a Indian; he ain't formed for society. This don't signify to a Spotted Baby; *he* ain't formed for society,—I am."

Nobody never could make out what Chops done with his money. He had a good salary, down on the drum every Saturday as the day came round, besides having the run of his teeth,—and he was a woodpecker to eat,—but all dwarfs are. The sarser was a little income, bringing him in so many half-pence that he'd carry 'em, for a week together, tied up in a pocket-handkercher. And yet he never had money. And it couldn't be the Fat Lady from Norfolk, as was once supposed; because it stands to reason that when you have a animosity towards a Indian which makes you grind your teeth at him to his face, and which can hardly hold you from goosing him audible when he's going through his war-dance,—it stands to reason you wouldn't under them circumstances deprive yourself to support that Indian in the lap of luxury.

Most unexpected, the mystery came out one day at Egham races. The public was shy of bein pulled in, and Chops was ringin his little bell out of his drawin-room winder, and was snarlin to me over his shoulder as he kneeled down with his legs out at the back door,—for he couldn't be shoved into his house without kneeling down, and the premises wouldn't accommodate his legs,—was snarlin: "Here's a precious public for you; why the devil don't they tumble up?" when a man in the crowd holds up a carrier-pigeon and cries out: "If there's any person here as has got a ticket, the Lottery's just drawd, and the number as has come up for the great prize is three, seven, forty-two! Three, seven, forty-two!" I was givin the man to the furies myself, for calling of the public's attention,—for the public will turn away, at any time, to look at anything in preference to the thing showed 'em; and if you doubt it, get 'em together for any individual purpose on the face of the earth, and send only two people in late and see if the whole company ain't far more interested in taking particular notice of them two than you,—I say I wasn't best pleased with the man for callin out, wasn't blessin him in my own mind, when I see Chops's little bell fly out of the winder at a old lady, and he gets up and kicks his box over, exposin the whole secret, and he catches hold of the calves of my legs and he says to me: "Carry me into the wan, Toby, and throw a pail of water over me, or I'm a dead man, for I'm come into my property!"

Twelve thousand odd hundred pounds was Chops's winnins. He had bought a half-ticket for the twenty-five thousand prize, and it had come up. The first use he made of his property was to offer to fight the Wild Indian for five hundred pound a side, him with a poisoned darnin-needle and the Indian with a club; but the Indian being in want of backers to that amount, it went no further.

Arter he had been mad for a week—in a state of mind, in short, in which, if I had let him sit on the organ for only two minutes, I believe he would have bust—but we kept the organ from him—Mr. Chops come round and behaved liberal and beautiful to all. He then sent for a young man he knowed, as had a wery genteel appearance and was a Bonnet at a gaming-booth (most respectable brought up, father havin been imminent in the livery-stable line, but unfort'nate in a commercial crisis through paintin a old gray, ginger-bay, and sellin him with a pedigree), and Mr. Chops said this to Bonnet, who said his name was Normandy, which it wasn't:—

"Normandy, I'm going into society. Will you go with me?"

Says Normandy: "Do I understand you, Mr. Chops, to hintimate that the 'ole of the expenses of that move will be borne by yourself?"

"Correct," says Mr. Chops. "And you shall have a princely allowance too."

The Bonnet lifted Mr. Chops upon a chair to shake hands with him, and replied in poetry, his eyes seemingly full of tears:—

"My boat is on the shore,
And my bark is on the sea,
And I do not ask for more,
But I'll go—along with thee."

They went into society, in a chaise and four grays, with silk jackets. They took lodgings in Pall Mall, London, and they blazed away.

In consequence of a note that was brought to Bartlemy Fair in the autumn of next year by a servant, most wonderful got up in milk-white cords and tops, I cleaned myself and went to Pall Mall, one evening appinted. The gentlemen was at their wine arter dinner, and Mr. Chops's eyes was more fixed in that Ed of his than I thought good for him. There was three of 'em (in company, I mean), and I knowed the third well. When last met, he had on a white Roman shirt, and a bishop's mitre covered with leopard-skin, and played the clarionet all wrong, in a band, at a wild-beast show.

This gent took on not to know me, and Mr. Chops said: "Gentlemen, this is an old friend of former days"; and Normandy looked at me through a eyeglass, and said, "Magsman, glad to see ye!" which I'll take my oath he wasn't. Mr. Chops, to get him convenient to the table, had his chair on a throne, much of the form of George Fourth's in the canvas, but he hardly appeared to me to be King there in any other pint of view, for his two gentlemen ordered about like emperors. They was all dressed like May-day—gorgeous!—and as to wine, they swam in all sorts.

I made the round of the bottles, first separate (to say I had done it), and then tried two of 'em as half-and-half, then t'other two. Altogether, I passed a pleasant evenin, but with a tendency to feel muddled, until I considered it good manners to get up and say: "Mr. Chops, the best of friends must part. I thank you for the wariety of foreign drains you have stood so 'ansome. I looks towards you in red wine, and I takes my leave." Mr. Chops replied: "If you'll just hitch me out of this over your right arm, Magsman, and carry me down stairs, I'll see you out." I said I couldn't think of such a thing, but he would have it, so I lifted him off his throne. He smelt strong of Madeary, and I couldn't help thinking, as I carried him down, that it was like carrying a large bottle full of wine, with a rayther ugly stopper, a good deal out of proportion.

When I set him on the door-mat in the hall, he kept me close to him by holding on to my coat-collar, and he whispers:—

"I ain't 'appy, Magsman."

"What's on your mind, Mr. Chops?"

"They don't use me well. They ain't graceful to me. They puts me on the mantel-piece when I won't have in more Champagne-wine, and they locks me in the sideboard when I won't give up my property."

"Git rid of 'em, Mr. Chops."

"I can't. We're in society together, and what would society say?"

"Come out of society," says I.

"I can't. You don't know what you're talking about. When you have once got into society, you mustn't come out of it."

"Then, if you'll excuse the freedom, Mr. Chops," was my remark, shaking my ed grave, "I think it's a pity you ever went in."

Mr. Chops shook that deep Ed of his to a surprisin extent, and slapped it half a dozen times with his hand, and with more wice than I thought were in him. Then he says: "You're a good feller, but you don't understand. Good night, go long. Magsman, the little man will now walk three times around the Cairawan, and retire behind the curtain." The last I see of him on that occasion was his tryin, on the extremest werge of insensibility, to climb up the stairs, one by one, with his hands and knees. They'd have been much too steep for him if he had been sober; but he wouldn't be helped.

It warn't long after that, that I read in the newspaper of Mr. Chops's being presented at court. It was printed: "It will be recollected"—and I've noticed in my life that it is sure to be printed that it *will* be recollected whenever it won't—"that Mr. Chops is the individual of small stature whose brilliant success in the last State Lottery attracted so much attention." "Well," I said to myself, "such is life! He has been and done it in earnest at last! He has astonished George the Fourth!"

On account of which I had that canvas new painted, him with a bag of money in his hand, a presentin it to George the Fourth, and a lady in ostrich feathers fallin in love with him in a bagwig, sword, and buckles correct.

I took the house as is the subject of present inquiries—though not the honor of being acquainted—and I run Magsman's Amusements in it thirteen months—sometimes one thing, sometimes another, sometimes nothin particular, but always all the canvases outside. One night, when we had played the last company out, which was a shy company through its raining heavens hard, I was takin a pipe in the one pair back, along with the young man with the toes, which I had taken on for a month (though he never drawed—except on paper), and I heard a kickin at the street door. "Halloa!" I says to the young man, "what's up?" He rubs his eyebrows with his toes, and he says, "I cant imagine, Mr. Magsman,"—which he never could imagine nothin, and was monotonous company.

The noise not leavin off, I laid down my pipe, and I took up a candle, and I went down and opened the door. I looked out into the street; but nothin could I see, and nothin was I aware of, until I turned round quick, because some creeter run between my legs into the passage. There was Mr. Chops!

"Magsman," he says, "take me on the hold terms, and you've got me; if it's done, say done!"

I was all of a maze, but I said, "Done, sir."

"Done to your done, and double done!" says he. "Have you got a bit of supper in the house?"

Bearin in mind them sparklin warieties of foreign drains as we'd guzzled away at in Pall Mall, I was ashamed to offer him cold sassages and gin-and-water; but he took 'em both and took 'em free; havin a chair for his table, and sittin down at it on a stool, like hold times,—I all of a maze all the while.

It was arter he had made a clean sweep of the sassages (beef, and to the best of my calculations two pounds and a quarter), that the wisdom as was in that little man began to come out of him like perspiration.

"Magsman," he says, "look upon me?—You see afore you one as has both gone into society, and come out."

"O, you *are* out of it, Mr. Chops? How did you get out, sir?"

"SOLD OUT!" says he. You never saw the like of the wisdom as his Ed expressed, when he made use of them two words.

"My friend Magsman, I'll impart to you a discovery I've made. It's wallable; it's cost twelve thousand five hundred pound; it may do you good in life. The secret of this matter is, that it ain't so much that a person goes into society, as that society goes into a person."

Not exactly keeping up with his meanin, I shook my ed, put on a deep look, and said, "You're right there, Mr. Chops."

"Magsman," he says, twitchin me by the leg, "society has gone into me to the tune of every penny of my property."

I felt that I went pale, and though not naturally a bold speaker, I couldn't hardly say, "Where's Normandy?"

"Bolted,—with the plate," said Mr. Chops.

"And t'other one?"—meaning him as formerly wore the bishop's mitre.

"Bolted,—with the jewels," said Mr. Chops.

I sat down and looked at him, and he stood up and looked at me.

"Magsman," he says, and he seemed to myself to get wiser as he got hoarser, "society, taken in the lump, is all dwarfs. At the court of Saint James they was all a doin my bisness—all a goin three times round the Cairawan, in the hold Court suits and properties. Elsewhere, they was most of 'em ringing their little bells out of makebelieves. Everywheres, the sarser was a goin round—Magsman, the sarser is the universal institution!"

I perceived, you understand, that he was soured by his misfortuns, and I felt for Mr. Chops.

"As to Fat Ladies," says he, giving his Ed a tremendious one agin the wall, "there's lots of *them* in society, and worse than the original. *Hers* was a outrage upon taste—simply a outrage upon taste—awakin contempt—carryin its own punishment in the form of a Indian!" Here he giv himself another tremendious one. "But *theirs*, Magsman, *theirs* is mercenary outrages. Lay in Cashmere shawls, buy bracelets, strew 'em and a lot of 'andsome fans and things about your rooms, let it be known that you give away like water to all as come to admire, and the Fat Ladies that don't exhibit for so much down upon the drum will come from all the pints of the compass to flock about you, whatever you are. They'll drill holes in your 'art, Magsman, like a cullender. And when you've no more left to give, they'll laugh at you to your face, and leave you to have your bones picked dry by wulturs, like the dead Wild Ass of the Prayries that you deserve to be!" Here he giv himself the most tremendious one of all, and dropped.

I thought he was gone. His Ed was so heavy, and he knocked it so hard, and he fell so stony, and the sassagereal disturbance in him must have been so immense, that I thought he was gone. But he soon come round with care, and he sat up on the floor, and he said to me, with wisdom comin out of his eyes, if ever it come,—

"Magsman! The most material difference between the two states of existence through which your unappy friend has passed,"—he reached out his poor little hand, and his tears dropped down on the mustache which it was a credit to him to have done his best to grow, but it is not in mortals to command success,—"the difference is this: When I was out of society, I was paid light for being seen. When I went into society, I paid heavy for being seen. I prefer the former, even if I wasn't forced upon it. Give me out through the trumpet, in the old way, to-morrow."

After that, he slid into the line again as easy as if he had been iled all over. But the organ was kep from him, and no allusions was ever made, when a company was in, to his property. He got wiser every day; his views of society and the public was luminous, bewilderin, awful; and his Ed got bigger and bigger as his wisdom expanded it.

He took well, and pulled 'em in most excellent for nine weeks. At the expiration of that period, when his Ed was a sight, he expressed one evening, the last company havin been turned out, and the doors shut, a wish to have a little music.

"Mr. Chops," I said (I never dropped the "Mr." with him; the world might do it, but not me),—"Mr. Chops, are you sure as you are in a state of mind and body to sit upon the organ?"

His answer was this: "Toby, when next met with on the tramp, I forgive her and the Indian. And I am."

It was with fear and tremblin that I began to turn the handle; but he sat like a lamb. It will be my belief to my dying day, that I see his Ed expand as he sat; you may therefore judge how great his thoughts was. He sat out all the changes, and then he come off.

"Toby," he says with a quiet smile, "the little man will now walk three times round the Cairawan, and then retire behind the curtain."

When we called him in the mornin we found he had gone into much better society than mine or Pall Mall's. I give Mr. Chops as comfortable a funeral as lay in my power, followed myself as chief, and had the George the Fourth canvas carried first, in the form of a banner. But the house was so dismal afterwards, that I give it up, and took to the wan again.

WAKEFIELD.
BY NATHANIEL HAWTHORNE.

IN some old magazine or newspaper, I recollect a story, told as truth, of a man—let us call him Wakefield—who absented himself for a long time from his wife. The fact, thus abstractedly stated, is not very uncommon, nor—without a proper distinction of circumstances—to be condemned either as naughty or nonsensical. Howbeit, this, though far from the most aggravated, is perhaps the strangest instance, on record, of marital delinquency; and, moreover, as remarkable a freak as may be found in the whole list of human oddities. The wedded couple lived in London. The man, under pretence of going a journey, took lodgings in the next street to his own house, and there, unheard of by his wife or friends, and without the shadow of a reason for such self-banishment, dwelt upward of twenty years. During that period he beheld his home every day, and frequently the forlorn Mrs. Wakefield. And after so great a gap in his matrimonial felicity,—when his death was reckoned certain, his estate settled, his name dismissed from memory, and his wife, long, long ago, resigned to her autumnal widowhood,—he entered the door one evening, quietly, as from a day's absence, and became a loving spouse till death.

This outline is all that I remember. But the incident, though of the purest originality, unexampled, and probably never to be repeated, is one, I think, which appeals to the generous sympathies of mankind. We know, each for himself, that none of us would perpetrate such a folly, yet feel as if some other might. To my own contemplations, at least, it has often recurred, always exciting wonder, but with a sense that the story must be true, and a conception of its hero's character. Whenever any subject so forcibly affects the mind, time is well spent in thinking of it. If the reader choose, let him do his own meditation; or if he prefer to ramble with me through the twenty years of Wakefield's vagary, I bid him welcome; trusting that there will be a pervading spirit and a moral, even should we fail to find them, done up neatly, and condensed into the final sentence. Thought has always its efficacy, and every striking incident its moral.

What sort of man was Wakefield? We are free to shape out our own idea, and call it by his name. He was now in the meridian of life; his matrimonial affections, never violent, were sobered into a calm, habitual sentiment; of all husbands, he was likely to be the most constant, because a certain sluggishness would keep his heart at rest, wherever it might be placed. He was intellectual, but not actively so; his mind occupied itself in long and lazy musings, that tended to no purpose, or had not vigor to attain it; his thoughts were seldom so energetic as to seize hold of words. Imagination, in the proper meaning of the term, made no part of Wakefield's gifts. With a cold but not depraved nor wandering heart, and a mind never feverish with riotous thoughts, nor perplexed with originality, who could have anticipated that our friend would entitle himself to a foremost place among the doers of eccentric deeds? Had his acquaintances been asked who was the man in London the surest to perform nothing to-day which should be remembered on the morrow, they would have thought of Wakefield. Only the wife of his bosom might have hesitated. She, without having analyzed his character, was partly aware of a quiet selfishness, that had rusted into his inactive mind,—of a peculiar sort of vanity, the most uneasy attribute about him,—of a disposition to craft, which had seldom produced more positive effects than the keeping of petty secrets, hardly worth revealing,—and, lastly, of what she called a little strangeness, sometimes, in the good man. This latter quality is indefinable, and perhaps non-existent.

Let us now imagine Wakefield bidding adieu to his wife. It is the dusk of an October evening. His equipment is a drab great-coat, a hat covered with an oil-cloth, top boots, an umbrella in one hand and a small portmanteau in the other. He has informed Mrs. Wakefield that he is to take the night coach into the country. She would fain inquire the length of his journey, its object, and the probable time of his return; but, indulgent to his harmless love of mystery, interrogates him only by a look. He tells her not to expect him positively by the return coach, nor to be alarmed should he tarry three or four days; but, at all events, to look for him at supper on Friday evening. Wakefield himself, be it considered, has no suspicion of what is before him. He holds out his hand; she gives her own, and meets his parting kiss, in the matter-of-course way of a ten years' matrimony; and forth goes the middle-aged Mr. Wakefield, almost resolved to perplex his good lady by a whole week's absence. After the door has closed behind him, she perceives it thrust partly open, and a vision of her husband's face, through the aperture, smiling on her, and gone in a moment. For the time, this little incident is dismissed without a thought. But, long afterward, when she has been more years a widow than a wife, that smile recurs, and flickers across all her reminiscences of Wakefield's visage. In her many musings, she surrounds the original smile with a multitude of fantasies, which make it strange and awful; as, for instance, if she imagines him in a coffin, that parting look is frozen on his pale features; or, if she dreams of him in heaven, still his blessed spirit wears a quiet and crafty smile. Yet, for its sake, when all others have given him up for dead, she sometimes doubts whether she is a widow.

But our business is with the husband. We must hurry after him, along the street, ere he lose his individuality, and melt into the great mass of London life. It would be vain searching for him there. Let us follow close at his heels, therefore, until, after several superfluous turns and doublings, we find him comfortably established by the fireside of a small apartment, previously bespoken. He is in the next street to his own, and at his journey's end. He can scarcely trust his good fortune, in having got thither unperceived,— recollecting that, at one time, he was delayed by the throng, in the very focus of a lighted lantern; and, again, there were footsteps, that seemed to tread behind his own, distinct from the multitudinous tramp around him; and, anon, he heard a voice shouting afar, and fancied that it called his name. Doubtless a dozen busybodies had been watching him, and told his wife the whole affair. Poor Wakefield! Little knowest thou thine own insignificance in this great world! No mortal eye but mine has traced thee. Go quietly to thy bed, foolish man; and, on the morrow, if thou wilt be wise, get thee home to good Mrs. Wakefield, and tell her the truth. Remove not thyself, even for a little week, from thy place in her chaste bosom. Were she, for a single moment, to deem thee dead, or lost, or lastingly divided from her, thou wouldst be woefully conscious of a change in thy true wife, forever after. It is perilous to make a chasm in human affections; not that they gape so long and wide, but so quickly close again!

Almost repenting of his frolic, or whatever it may be termed, Wakefield lies down betimes, and, starting from his first nap, spreads forth his arms into the wide and solitary waste of the unaccustomed bed. "No," thinks he, gathering the bedclothes about him, "I will not sleep alone another night."

In the morning, he rises earlier than usual, and sets himself to consider what he really means to do. Such are his loose and rambling modes of thought, that he has taken this very singular step, with the consciousness of a purpose, indeed, but without being able to define it sufficiently for his own contemplation. The vagueness of the project, and the convulsive effort with which he plunges into the execution of it, are equally characteristic of a feeble-minded man. Wakefield sifts his ideas, however, as minutely as he may, and finds himself curious to know the progress of matters at home,— how his exemplary wife will endure her widowhood of a week; and, briefly, how the little sphere of creatures and circumstances, in which he was a central object, will be affected by his removal. A morbid vanity, therefore, lies nearest the bottom of the affair. But how is he to attain his ends? Not, certainly, by keeping close in this comfortable lodging, where, though he slept and awoke in the next street to his home, he is as effectually abroad as if the stage-coach had been whirling him away all night. Yet, should he reappear, the whole project is knocked in the head. His poor brains being hopelessly puzzled with this dilemma, he at length ventures out, partly resolving to cross the head of the street, and send one hasty glance toward his forsaken domicile. Habit—for he is a man of habits—takes him by the hand, and guides him, wholly unaware, to his own door, where, just at the critical moment, he is aroused by the scraping of his foot upon the step. Wakefield! whither are you going?

At that instant, his fate was turning on the pivot. Little dreaming of the doom to which his first backward step devotes him, he hurries away, breathless with agitation hitherto unfelt, and hardly dares turn his head at the distant corner. Can it be that nobody caught sight of him? Will not the whole household—the decent Mrs. Wakefield, the smart maid-servant, and the dirty little footboy—raise a hue and cry, through London streets, in pursuit of their fugitive lord and master? Wonderful escape! He gathers courage to pause and look homeward, but is perplexed with a sense of change about the familiar edifice, such as affects us all when, after a separation of months or years, we again see some hill or lake, or work of art, with which we were friends of old. In ordinary cases, this indescribable impression is caused by the comparison and contrast between our imperfect reminiscences and the reality. In Wakefield, the magic of a single night has wrought a similar transformation, because, in that brief period, a great moral change has been effected. But this is a secret from himself. Before leaving the spot, he catches a far and momentary glimpse of his wife, passing athwart the front window, with her face turned toward the head of the street. The crafty nincompoop takes to his heels, scared with the idea that, among a thousand such atoms of mortality, her eye must have detected him. Right glad is his heart, though his brain be somewhat dizzy, when he finds himself by the coal fire of his lodgings.

So much for the commencement of this long whim-wham. After the initial conception, and the stirring up of the man's sluggish temperament to put it in practice, the whole matter evolves itself in a natural train. We may suppose him, as the result of deep deliberation, buying a new wig, of reddish hair, and selecting sundry garments, in a fashion unlike his customary suit of brown, from a Jew's old-clothes bag. It is accomplished. Wakefield is another man. The new system being now established, a retrograde movement to the old would be almost as difficult as the step that placed him in his unparalleled position. Furthermore, he is rendered obstinate by a sulkiness, occasionally incident to his temper, and brought on, at present, by the inadequate sensation which he conceives to have been produced in the bosom of Mrs. Wakefield. He will not go back until she be frightened half to death. Well; twice or thrice has she passed before his sight, each time with a heavier step, a paler cheek, and a more anxious brow; and in the third week of his non-appearance, he detects a portent of evil entering the house, in the guise of an apothecary. Next day, the knocker is muffled. Toward nightfall comes the chariot of a physician, and deposits its big-wigged and solemn burden at Wakefield's door, whence, after a quarter of an hour's visit, he emerges, perchance the herald of a funeral. Dear woman! Will she die? By this time, Wakefield is excited to something like energy of feeling, but still lingers away from his wife's bedside, pleading with his conscience, that she must not be disturbed at such a juncture. If aught else restrains him, he does not know it. In the course of a few weeks, she gradually recovers; the crisis is over; her heart is sad, perhaps, but quiet; and, let him return soon or late, it will never be feverish for him again. Such ideas glimmer through the mist of Wakefield's mind, and render him indistinctly conscious that an almost impassable gulf divides his hired apartment from his former home. "It is but in the next street!" he sometimes says. Fool! it is in another world. Hitherto, he has put off his return from one particular day to another; henceforward, he leaves the precise time undetermined. Not to-morrow,—probably next week,—pretty soon. Poor man! The dead have nearly as much chance of revisiting their earthly homes, as the self-banished Wakefield.

Would that I had a folio to write, instead of an article of a dozen pages! Then might I exemplify how an influence, beyond our control, lays its strong hand on every deed which we do, and weaves its consequences into an iron tissue of necessity. Wakefield is spellbound. We must leave him, for ten years or so, to haunt around his house, without once crossing the threshold, and to be faithful to his wife, with all the affection of which his heart is capable, while he is slowly fading out of hers. Long since, it must be remarked, he has lost the perception of singularity in his conduct.

Now for a scene! Amid the throng of a London street, we distinguish a man, now waxing elderly, with few characteristics to attract careless observers, yet bearing, in his whole aspect, the handwriting of no common fate, for such as have the skill to read it. He is meagre; his low and narrow forehead is deeply wrinkled; his eyes, small and lustreless, sometimes wander apprehensively about him, but oftener seem to look inward. He bends his head, and moves with an indescribable obliquity of gait, as if unwilling to display his full front to the world. Watch him long enough to see what we have described, and you will allow that circumstances, which often produce remarkable men from nature's ordinary handiwork, have produced one such here. Next, leaving him to sidle along the footwalk, cast your eyes in the opposite direction, where a portly female, considerably in the wane of life, with a prayer-book in her hand, is proceeding to yonder church. She has the placid mien of settled widowhood. Her regrets have either died away, or have become so essential to her heart that they would be poorly exchanged for joy. Just as the lean man and the well-conditioned woman are passing, a slight obstruction occurs, and brings these two figures directly in contact. Their hands touch; the pressure of the crowd forces her bosom against his shoulder; they stand face to face, staring into each other's eyes. After a ten years' separation, thus Wakefield meets his wife!

The throng eddies away, and carries them asunder. The sober widow, resuming her former pace, proceeds to church, but pauses in the portal, and throws a perplexed glance along the street. She passes in, however, opening her prayer-book as she goes. And the man! with so wild a face that busy and selfish London stands to gaze after him, he hurries to his lodgings, bolts the door, and throws himself upon the bed. The latent feelings of years break out; his feeble mind acquires a brief energy from their strength; all the miserable strangeness of his life is revealed to him at a glance: and he cries out passionately, "Wakefield! Wakefield! you are mad!"

Perhaps he was so. The singularity of his situation must have so moulded him to himself, that, considered in regard to his fellow-creatures and the business of life, he could not be said to possess his right mind. He had contrived, or rather he had happened, to dissever himself from the world,—to vanish,—to give up his place and privileges with living men, without being admitted among the dead. The life of a hermit is nowise parallel to his. He was in the bustle of the city, as of old; but the crowd swept by, and saw him not; he was, we may figuratively say, always beside his wife, and at his hearth, yet must never feel the warmth of the one, nor the affection of the other. It was Wakefield's unprecedented fate to retain his original share of human sympathies, and to be still involved in human interests, while he had lost his reciprocal influence on them. It would be a most curious speculation to trace out the effect of such circumstances on his heart and intellect, separately, and in unison. Yet, changed as he was, he would seldom be conscious of it, but deem himself the same man as ever; glimpses of the truth, indeed, would come, but only for the moment; and still he would keep saying, "I shall soon go back!"—nor reflect that he had been saying so for twenty years.

I conceive, also, that these twenty years would appear, in the retrospect, scarcely longer than the week to which Wakefield had at first limited his absence. He would look on the affair as no more than an interlude in the main business of his life. When, after a little while more, he should deem it time to re-enter his parlor, his wife would clap her hands for joy, on beholding the middle-aged Mr. Wakefield. Alas, what a mistake! Would Time but await the close of our favorite follies, we should be young men, all of us, and till Doomsday.

One evening, in the twentieth year since he vanished, Wakefield is taking his customary walk toward the dwelling which he still calls his own. It is a gusty night of autumn, with frequent showers, that patter down upon the pavement, and are gone, before a man can put up his umbrella. Pausing near the house, Wakefield discerns, through the parlor windows of the second floor, the red glow, and the glimmer and fitful flash, of a comfortable fire. On the ceiling appears a grotesque shadow of good Mrs. Wakefield. The cap, the nose and chin, and the broad waist form an admirable caricature, which dances, moreover, with the up-flickering and down-sinking blaze, almost too merrily for the shade of an elderly widow. At this instant, a shower chances to fall, and is driven, by the unmannerly gust, full into Wakefield's face and bosom. He is quite penetrated with its autumnal chill. Shall he stand, wet and shivering here, when his own hearth has a good fire to warm him, and his own wife will run to fetch the gray coat and small-clothes, which, doubtless, she has kept carefully in the closet of their bedchamber? No! Wakefield is no such fool. He ascends the steps,—heavily!—for twenty years have stiffened his legs, since he came down,—but he knows it not. Stay, Wakefield! Would you go to the sole home that is left you? Then step into your grave! The door opens. As he passes in, we have a parting glimpse of his visage, and recognize the crafty smile which was the precursor of the little joke that he has ever since been playing off at his wife's expense. How unmercifully has he quizzed the poor woman! Well, a good night's rest to Wakefield!

This happy event—supposing it to be such—could only have occurred at an unpremeditated moment. We will not follow our friend across the threshold. He has left us much food for thought, a portion of which shall lend its wisdom to a moral, and be shaped into a figure. Amid the seeming confusion of our mysterious world, individuals are so nicely adjusted to a system, and systems to one another and to a whole, that, by stepping aside for a moment, a man exposes himself to a fearful risk of losing his place forever. Like Wakefield, he may become, as it were, the Outcast of the Universe.

MURDER,
CONSIDERED AS ONE OF THE FINE ARTS.
BY THOMAS DE QUINCEY.

WE have all heard of a Society for the Promotion of Vice, of the Hell-Fire Club, etc. At Brighton, I think it was, that a Society was formed for the Suppression of Virtue. That Society was itself suppressed; but I am sorry to say that another exists in London, of a character still more atrocious. In tendency, it may be denominated a Society for the Encouragement of Murder; but, according to their own delicate εὐφημισμός, it is styled, The Society of Connoisseurs in Murder. They profess to be curious in homicide; amateurs and dilettanti in the various modes of bloodshed; and, in short, murder-fanciers. Every fresh atrocity of that class, which the police annals of Europe bring up, they meet and criticise as they would a picture, statue, or other work of art. But I need not trouble myself with any attempt to describe the spirit of their proceedings, as you will collect *that* much better from one of the monthly lectures read before the society last year. This has fallen into my hands, accidentally, in spite of all the vigilance exercised to keep their transactions from the public eye. The publication of it will alarm them; and my purpose is that it should. For I would much rather put them down quietly, by an appeal to public opinion, than by such an exposure of names as would follow an appeal to Bow Street; which last appeal, however, if this should fail, I must positively resort to.

LECTURE.

GENTLEMEN,—I have had the honor to be appointed by your committee to the trying task of reading the Williams Lecture on Murder, considered as one of the Fine Arts; a task which might be easy enough three or four centuries ago, when the art was little understood, and few great models had been exhibited; but in this age, when masterpieces of excellence have been executed by professional men, it must be evident that, in the style of criticism applied to them, the public will look for something of a corresponding improvement. Practice and theory must advance *pari passu*. People begin to see that something more goes to the composition of a fine murder than two blockheads to kill and be killed,—a knife,—a purse,—and a dark lane. Design, gentlemen, grouping, light and shade, poetry, sentiment, are now deemed indispensable to attempts of this nature. Mr. Williams has exalted the ideal of murder to all of us; and to me, therefore, in particular, has deepened the arduousness of my task. Like Æschylus or Milton in poetry, like Michael Angelo in painting, he has carried his art to a point of colossal sublimity; and, as Mr. Wordsworth observes, has in a manner "created the taste by which he is to be enjoyed." To sketch the history of the art, and to examine its principles critically, now remains as a duty for the connoisseur, and for judges of quite another stamp from his Majesty's Judges of Assize.

Before I begin, let me say a word or two to certain prigs, who affect to speak of our society as if it were in some degree immoral in its tendency. Immoral! God bless my soul, gentlemen, what is it that people mean? I am for morality, and always shall be, and for virtue and all that; and I do affirm, and always shall (let what will come of it), that murder is an improper line of conduct, highly improper; and I do not stick to assert that any man who deals in murder must have very incorrect ways of thinking, and truly inaccurate principles; and so far from aiding and abetting him by pointing out his victim's hiding-place, as a great moralist[A] of Germany declared it to be every good man's duty to do, I would subscribe one shilling and sixpence to have him apprehended, which is more by eighteen-pence than the most eminent moralists have subscribed for that purpose. But what then? Everything in this world has two handles. Murder, for instance, may be laid hold of by its moral handle (as it generally is in the pulpit, and at the Old Bailey); and *that*, I confess, is its weak side; or it may also be treated *æsthetically*, as the Germans call it, that is, in relation to good taste.

To illustrate this, I will urge the authority of three eminent persons, namely, S. T. Coleridge, Aristotle, and Mr. Howship the surgeon. To begin with S. T. C. One night, many years ago, I was drinking tea with him in Berners Street (which, by the way, for a short street, has been uncommonly fruitful in men of genius). Others were there besides myself; and amidst some carnal considerations of tea and toast, we were all imbibing a dissertation on Plotinus from the attic lips of S. T. C. Suddenly a cry arose of "*Fire,— fire!*" upon which all of us, master and disciples, Plato and οἱ περὶ τον Πλάτωνα, rushed out, eager for the spectacle. The fire was in Oxford Street, at a piano-forte maker's; and, as it promised to be a conflagration of merit, I was sorry that my engagements forced me away from Mr. Coleridge's party before matters were come to a crisis. Some days after, meeting with my Platonic host, I reminded him of the case, and begged to know how that very promising exhibition had terminated. "O sir," said he, "it turned out so ill, that we damned it unanimously!" Now, does any man suppose that Mr. Coleridge,—who, for all he is too fat to be a person of active virtue, is undoubtedly a worthy Christian,—that this good S. T. C., I say, was an incendiary, or capable of wishing any ill to the poor man and his piano-fortes (many of them, doubtless, with the additional keys)? On the contrary, I know him to be that sort of man, that I durst stake my life upon it he would have worked an engine in a case of necessity, although rather of the fattest for such fiery trials of his virtue. But how stood the case? Virtue was in no request. On the arrival of the fire-engines, morality had devolved wholly on the insurance office. This being the case, he had a right to gratify his taste. He had left his tea. Was he to have nothing in return?

I contend that the most virtuous man, under the premises stated, was entitled to make a luxury of the fire, and to hiss it, as he would any other performance that raised expectations in the public mind, which afterwards it disappointed. Again, to cite another great authority, what says the Stagyrite? He (in the Fifth Book, I think it is, of his Metaphysics) describes what he calls κλεπτὴν τέλειον, i.e. *a perfect thief*; and, as to Mr. Howship, in a work of his on Indigestion, he makes no scruple to talk with admiration of a certain ulcer which he had seen, and which he styles "a beautiful ulcer." Now will any man pretend that, abstractly considered, a thief could appear to Aristotle a perfect character, or that Mr. Howship could be enamored of an ulcer? Aristotle, it is well known, was himself so very moral a character that, not content with writing his Nichomachéan Ethics, in one volume octavo, he also wrote another system, called *Magna Moralia*, or Big Ethics. Now, it is impossible that a man who composes any ethics at all, big or little, should admire a thief *per se*; and, as to Mr. Howship, it is well known that he makes war upon all ulcers, and, without suffering himself to be seduced by their charms, endeavors to banish them from the county of Middlesex. But the truth is, that, however objectionable *per se*, yet, relatively to others of their class, both a thief and an ulcer may have infinite degrees of merit. They are both imperfections, it is true; but to be imperfect being their essence, the very greatness of their imperfection becomes their perfection. *Spartam nactus es, hanc exorna.* A thief like Autolycus or Mr. Barrington, and a grim phagedænic ulcer, superbly defined, and running regularly through all its natural stages, may no less justly be regarded as ideals after *their* kind, than the most faultless moss-rose amongst flowers, in its progress from bud to "bright consummate flower"; or, amongst human flowers, the most magnificent young female, apparelled in the pomp of womanhood. And thus not only the ideal of an inkstand may be imagined (as Mr. Coleridge demonstrated in his celebrated correspondence with Mr. Blackwood), in which, by the way, there is not so much, because an inkstand is a laudable sort of thing, and a valuable member of society; but even imperfection itself may have its ideal or perfect state.

Really, gentlemen, I beg pardon for so much philosophy at one time, and now let me apply it. When a murder is in the paulo-post-futurum tense, and a rumor of it comes to our ears, by all means let us treat it morally. But suppose it over and done, and that you can say of it, Τετέλεςαι, or (in that adamantine molossus of Medea) εἰρξαςαι; suppose the poor murdered man to be out of his pain, and the rascal that did it off like a shot, nobody knows whither; suppose, lastly, that we have done our best, by putting out our legs to trip up the fellow in his flight, but all to no purpose,—"abiit, evasit," etc.,—why, then, I say, what's the use of any more virtue? Enough has been given to morality; now comes the turn of Taste and the Fine Arts. A sad thing it was, no doubt, very sad; but *we* can't mend it. Therefore let us make the best of a bad matter; and as it is impossible to hammer anything out of it for moral purposes, let us treat it æsthetically, and see if it will turn to account in that way. Such is the logic of a sensible man, and what follows? We dry up our tears, and have the satisfaction, perhaps, to discover that a transaction which, morally considered, was shocking, and without a leg to stand upon, when tried by principles of Taste, turns out to be a very meritorious performance. Thus all the world is pleased; the old proverb is justified, that it is an ill wind which blows nobody good; the amateur, from looking bilious and sulky, by too close an attention to virtue, begins to pick up his crumbs, and general hilarity prevails. Virtue has had her day; and henceforward, *Vertu* and Connoisseurship have leave to provide for themselves. Upon this principle, gentlemen, I propose to guide your studies, from Cain to Mr. Thurtell. Through this great gallery of murder, therefore, together let us wander hand in hand, in delighted admiration, while I endeavor to point your attention to the objects of profitable criticism.

———

The first murder is familiar to you all. As the inventor of murder, and the father of the art, Cain must have been a man of first-rate genius. All the Cains were men of genius. Tubal Cain invented tubes, I think, or some such thing. But, whatever were the originality and genius of the artist, every art was then in its infancy, and the works must be criticised with a recollection of that fact. Even Tubal's work would probably be little approved at this day in Sheffield; and therefore of Cain (Cain senior, I mean) it is no disparagement to say, that his performance was but so so. Milton, however, is supposed to have thought differently. By his way of relating the case, it should seem to have been rather a pet murder with him, for he retouches it with an apparent anxiety for its picturesque effect:—

"Whereat he inly raged; and, as they talk'd,
Smote him into the midriff with a stone
That beat out life: he fell; and, deadly pale,
Groan'd out his soul *with gushing blood effus'd*."
Par. Lost, B. XI.

Upon this, Richardson, the painter, who had an eye for effect, remarks as follows, in his Notes on Paradise Lost, p. 497: "It has been thought," says he, "that Cain beat (as the common saying is) the breath out of his brother's body with a great stone; Milton gives in to this, with the addition, however, of a large wound." In this place it was a judicious addition; for the rudeness of the weapon, unless raised and enriched by a warm, sanguinary coloring, has too much of the naked air of the savage school; as if the deed were perpetrated by a Polypheme without science, premeditation, or anything but a mutton bone. However, I am chiefly pleased with the improvement, as it implies that Milton was an amateur. As to Shakespeare, there never was a better; as his description of the murdered Duke of Gloucester, in Henry VI., of Duncan's, Banquo's, etc., sufficiently proves.

The foundation of the art having been once laid, it is pitiable to see how it slumbered without improvement for ages. In fact, I shall now be obliged to leap over all murders, sacred and profane, as utterly unworthy of notice, until long after the Christian era. Greece, even in the age of Pericles, produced no murder of the slightest merit; and Rome had too little originality of genius in any of the arts to succeed, where her model failed her. In fact, the Latin language sinks under the very idea of murder. "The man was murdered";—how will this sound in Latin? *Interfectus est, interemptus est,*—which simply expresses a homicide; and hence the Christian Latinity of the Middle Ages was obliged to introduce a new word, such as the feebleness of classic conceptions never ascended to. *Murdratus est,* says the sublimer dialect of Gothic ages. Meantime, the Jewish school of murder kept alive whatever was yet known in the art, and gradually transferred it to the Western World. Indeed the Jewish school was always respectable, even in the dark ages, as the case of Hugh of Lincoln shows, which was honored with the approbation of Chaucer, on occasion of another performance from the same school which he puts into the mouth of the Lady Abbess.

Recurring, however, for one moment to classical antiquity, I cannot but think that Catiline, Clodius, and some of that coterie would have made first-rate artists; and it is on all accounts to be regretted, that the priggism of Cicero robbed his country of the only chance she had for distinction in this line. As the *subject* of a murder, no person could have answered better than himself. Lord! how he would have howled with panic, if he had heard Cethegus under his bed. It would have been truly diverting to have listened to him; and satisfied I am, gentlemen, that he would have preferred the *utile* of creeping into a closet, or even into a *cloaca,* to the *honestum* of facing the bold artist.

To come now to the dark ages (by which we, that speak with precision, mean, *par excellence,* the tenth century, and the times immediately before and after), these ages ought naturally to be favorable to the art of murder, as they were to church architecture, to stained glass, etc.; and, accordingly, about the latter end of this period, there arose a great character in our art, I mean the Old Man of the Mountains. He was a shining light, indeed, and I need not tell you that the very word "assassin" is deduced from him. So keen an amateur was he, that on one occasion, when his own life was attempted by a favorite assassin, he was so much pleased with the talent shown, that, notwithstanding the failure of the artist, he created him a Duke upon the spot, with remainder to the female line, and settled a pension on him for three lives. Assassination is a branch of the art which demands a separate notice; and I shall devote an entire lecture to it. Meantime, I shall only observe how odd it is that this branch of the art has flourished by fits. It never rains, but it pours. Our own age can boast of some fine specimens; and about two centuries ago there was a most brilliant constellation of murders in this class. I need hardly say that I allude especially to those five splendid works,—the assassinations of William I., of Orange, of Henry IV., of France, of the Duke of Buckingham (which you will find excellently described in the letters published by Mr. Ellis, of the British Museum), of Gustavus Adolphus, and of Wallenstein. The King of Sweden's assassination, by the by, is doubted by many writers, Harte amongst others; but they are wrong. He was murdered; and I consider his murder unique in its excellence; for he was murdered at noonday, and on the field of battle,— a feature of original conception, which occurs in no other work of art that I remember. Indeed, all of these assassinations may be studied with profit by the advanced connoisseur. They are all of them *exemplaria*, of which one may say,—

"Nocturna versata manu, versate diurne";

especially *nocturna*.

In these assassinations of princes and statesmen, there is nothing to excite our wonder; important changes often depend on their deaths; and, from the eminence on which they stand, they are peculiarly exposed to the aim of every artist who happens to be possessed by the craving for scenical effect. But there is another class of assassinations, which has prevailed from an early period of the seventeenth century, that really *does* surprise me; I mean the assassination of philosophers. For, gentlemen, it is a fact that every philosopher of eminence for the two last centuries has either been murdered, or, at the least, been very near it; insomuch, that if a man calls himself a philosopher, and never had his life attempted, rest assured there is nothing in him; and against Locke's philosophy in particular, I think it an unanswerable objection (if we needed any) that, although he carried his throat about with him in this world for seventy-two years, no man ever condescended to cut it. As these cases of philosophers are not much known, and are generally good and well composed in their circumstances, I shall here read an excursus on that subject, chiefly by way of showing my own learning.

The first great philosopher of the seventeenth century (if we except Galileo) was Des Cartes; and if ever one could say of a man that he was all *but* murdered,—murdered within an inch,—one must say it of him. The case was this, as reported by Baillet in his *Vie De M. Des Cartes*, Tom. I. pp. 102-3. In the year 1621, when Des Cartes might be about twenty-six years old, he was touring about as usual (for he was as restless as a hyena), and, coming to the Elbe, either at Gluckstadt or at Hamburg, he took shipping for East Friezland: what he could want in East Friezland, no man has ever discovered; and perhaps he took this into consideration himself; for, on reaching Embden, he resolved to sail instantly for *West* Friezland; and, being very impatient of delay, he hired a bark, with a few mariners to navigate it. No sooner had he got out to sea, than he made a pleasing discovery, namely, that he had shut himself up in a den of murderers. His crew, says M. Baillet, he soon found out to be "des scélérats,"—not *amateurs*, gentlemen, as we are, but professional men,—the height of whose ambition at that moment was to cut his throat. But the story is too pleasing to be abridged; I shall give it, therefore, accurately, from the French of his biographer: "M. Des Cartes had no company but that of his servant, with whom he was conversing in French. The sailors, who took him for a foreign merchant, rather than a cavalier, concluded that he must have money about him. Accordingly they came to a resolution by no means advantageous to his purse. There is this difference, however, between sea-robbers and the robbers in forests, that the latter may, without hazard, spare the lives of their victims; whereas the other cannot put a passenger on shore in such a case without running the risk of being apprehended. The crew of M. Des Cartes arranged their measures with a view to evade any danger of that sort. They observed that he was a stranger from a distance, without acquaintance in the country, and that nobody would take any trouble to inquire about him, in case he should never come to hand, *quand il viendroit à manquer.*" Think, gentlemen, of these Friezland dogs discussing a philosopher as if he were a puncheon of rum. "His temper, they remarked, was very mild and patient; and, judging from the gentleness of his deportment, and the courtesy with which he treated themselves, that he could be nothing more than some green young man, they concluded that they should have all the easier task in disposing of his life. They made no scruple to discuss the whole matter in his presence, as not supposing that he understood any other language than that in which he conversed with his servant; and the amount of their deliberation was—to murder him, then to throw him into the sea, and to divide his spoils."

Excuse my laughing, gentlemen, but the fact is, I always *do* laugh when I think of this case,—two things about it seem so droll. One is, the horrid panic or "funk" (as the men of Eton call it) in which Des Cartes must have found himself upon hearing this regular drama sketched for his own death,—funeral,—succession and administration to his effects. But another thing which seems to me still more funny about this affair is, that if these Friezland hounds had been "game," we should have no Cartesian philosophy; and how we could have done without *that*, considering the world of books it has produced, I leave to any respectable trunk-maker to declare.

However, to go on; spite of his enormous funk, Des Cartes showed fight, and by that means awed these Anti-Cartesian rascals. "Finding," says M. Baillet, "that the matter was no joke, M. Des Cartes leaped upon his feet in a trice, assumed a stern countenance that these cravens had never looked for, and, addressing them in their own language, threatened to run them through on the spot if they dared to offer him any insult." Certainly, gentlemen, this would have been an honor far above the merits of such inconsiderable rascals,—to be spitted like larks upon a Cartesian sword; and therefore I am glad M. Des Cartes did not rob the gallows by executing his threat, especially as he could not possibly have brought his vessel to port, after he had murdered his crew; so that he must have continued to cruise forever in the Zuyder Zee, and would probably have been mistaken by sailors for the *Flying Dutchman*, homeward bound. "The spirit which M. Des Cartes manifested," says his biographer, "had the effect of magic on these wretches. The suddenness of their consternation struck their minds with a confusion which blinded them to their advantage, and they conveyed him to his destination as peaceably as he could desire."

Possibly, gentlemen, you may fancy that, on the model of Cæsar's address to his poor ferryman,—"*Cæsarem vehis et fortunas ejus*,"—M. Des Cartes needed only to have said, "Dogs, you cannot cut my throat, for you carry Des Cartes and his philosophy," and might safely have defied them to do their worst. A German emperor had the same notion, when, being cautioned to keep out of the way of a cannonading, he replied, "Tut! man. Did you ever hear of a cannon-ball that killed an emperor?" As to an emperor I cannot say, but a less thing has sufficed to smash a philosopher; and the next great philosopher of Europe undoubtedly *was* murdered. This was Spinosa.

I know very well the common opinion about him is, that he died in his bed. Perhaps he did, but he was murdered, for all that; and this I shall prove by a book published at Brussels, in the year 1731, entitled *La Vie de Spinosa; Par M. Jean Colerus*, with many additions, from a manuscript life, by one of his friends. Spinosa died on the 21st February, 1677, being then little more than forty-four years old. This, of itself, looks suspicious; and M. Jean admits, that a certain expression in the manuscript life of him would warrant the conclusion, "que sa mort n'a pas été tout-à-fait naturelle." Living in a damp country, and a sailor's country, like Holland, he may be thought to have indulged a good deal in grog, especially in punch,[B] which was then newly discovered. Undoubtedly he might have done so; but the fact is, that he did not. M. Jean calls him, "extrêmement sobre en son boire et en son manger." And though some wild stories were afloat about his using the juice of mandragora (p. 140), and opium (p. 144), yet neither of these articles appeared in his druggist's bill. Living, therefore, with such sobriety, how was it possible that he should die a natural death at forty-four? Hear his biographer's account: "Sunday morning, the 21st of February, before it was church time, Spinosa came down stairs and conversed with the master and mistress of the house." At this time, therefore, perhaps ten o'clock on Sunday morning, you see that Spinosa was alive and pretty well. But it seems "he had summoned from Amsterdam a certain physician, whom," says the biographer, "I shall not otherwise point out to notice than by these two letters, L. M. This L. M. had directed the people of the house to purchase an ancient cock, and to have him boiled forthwith, in order that Spinosa might take some broth about noon, which in fact he did, and ate some of the *old cock* with a good appetite, after the landlord and his wife had returned from church.

"In the afternoon L. M. stayed alone with Spinosa, the people of the house having returned to church; on coming out from which they learnt, with much surprise, that Spinosa had died about three o'clock, in the presence of L. M., who took his departure for Amsterdam the same evening, by the night boat, without paying the least attention to the deceased. No doubt he was the readier to dispense with these duties, as he had possessed himself of a ducatoon and a small quantity of silver, together with a silver-hafted knife, and had absconded with his pillage." Here you see, gentlemen, the murder is plain, and the manner of it. It was L. M. who murdered Spinosa for his money. Poor S. was an invalid, meagre and weak: as no blood was observed, L. M. no doubt threw him down and smothered him with pillows,—the poor man being already half suffocated by his infernal dinner. But who was L. M.? It surely never could be Lindley Murray; for I saw him at York in 1825; and besides, I do not think he would do such a thing; at least, not to a brother grammarian: for you know, gentlemen, that Spinosa wrote a very respectable Hebrew grammar.

Hobbes, but why, or on what principle, I never could understand, was not murdered. This was a capital oversight of the professional men in the seventeenth century; because in every light he was a fine subject for murder, except, indeed, that he was lean and skinny; for I can prove that he had money, and (what is very funny) he had no right to make the least resistance; for, according to himself, irresistible power creates the very highest species of right, so that it is rebellion of the blackest dye to refuse to be murdered, when a competent force appears to murder you. However, gentlemen, though he was not murdered, I am happy to assure you that (by his own account) he was three times very near being murdered. The first time was in the spring of 1640, when he pretends to have circulated a little manuscript on the king's behalf, against the Parliament; he never could produce this manuscript, by the by: but he says that, "Had not his Majesty dissolved the Parliament" (in May), "it had brought him into danger of his life." Dissolving the Parliament, however, was of no use; for, in November of the same year, the Long Parliament assembled, and Hobbes, a second time, fearing he should be murdered, ran away to France. This looks like the madness of John Dennis, who thought that Louis XIV. would never make peace with Queen Anne, unless he were given up to his vengeance; and actually ran away from the sea-coast in that belief. In France, Hobbes managed to take care of his throat pretty well for ten years; but at the end of that time, by way of paying court to Cromwell, he published his Leviathan. The old coward now began to "funk" horribly for the third time; he fancied the swords of the cavaliers were constantly at his throat, recollecting how they had served the Parliament ambassadors at the Hague and Madrid. "Tum," says he, in his dog-Latin life of himself,—

"Tum venit in mentem mihi Dorislaus et Ascham;
Tanquam proscripto terror ubique aderat."

And accordingly he ran home to England. Now, certainly, it is very true that a man deserved a cudgelling for writing Leviathan; and two or three cudgellings for writing a pentameter ending so villanously as, "terror ubique aderat"! But no man ever thought him worthy of anything beyond cudgelling. And, in fact, the whole story is a bounce of his own. For, in a most abusive letter which he wrote "to a learned person" (meaning Wallis the mathematician), he gives quite another account of the matter, and says (p. 8), he ran home "because he would not trust his safety with the French clergy"; insinuating that he was likely to be murdered for his religion, which would have been a high joke indeed,—Tom's being brought to the stake for religion.

Bounce or not bounce, however, certain it is, that Hobbes, to the end of his life, feared that somebody would murder him. This is proved by the story I am going to tell you: it is not from a manuscript, but (as Mr. Coleridge says) it is as good as manuscript; for it comes from a book now entirely forgotten, namely, "The Creed of Mr. Hobbes Examined; in a Conference between him and a Student in Divinity" (published about ten years before Hobbes's death). The book is anonymous, but it was written by Tennison, the same who, about thirty years after, succeeded Tillotson as Archbishop of Canterbury. The introductory anecdote is as follows: "A certain divine, it seems (no doubt Tennison himself), took an annual tour of one month to different parts of the island. In one of these excursions (1670) he visited the Peak in Derbyshire, partly in consequence of Hobbes's description of it. Being in that neighborhood, he could not but pay a visit to Buxton; and at the very moment of his arrival, he was fortunate enough to find a party of gentlemen dismounting at the inn door, amongst whom was a long, thin fellow, who turned out to be no less a person than Mr. Hobbes, who probably had ridden over from Chatsworth. Meeting so great a lion, a tourist, in search of the picturesque, could do no less than present himself in the character of bore. And luckily for this scheme, two of Mr. Hobbes's companions were suddenly summoned away by express; so that, for the rest of his stay at Buxton, he had Leviathan entirely to himself, and had the honor of bowsing with him in the evening. Hobbes, it seems, at first showed a good deal of stiffness, for he was shy of divines; but this wore off, and he became very sociable and funny, and they agreed to go into the bath together. How Tennison could venture to gambol in the same water with Leviathan, I cannot explain; but so it was: they frolicked about like two dolphins, though Hobbes must have been as old as the hills; and in those intervals wherein they abstained from swimming and plunging themselves" (i. e. diving) "they discoursed of many things relating to the Baths of the Ancients, and the Origine of Springs. When they had in this manner passed away an hour, they stepped out of the bath; and, having dried and cloathed themselves, they sate down in expectation of such a supper as the place afforded; designing to refresh themselves like the *Deipnosophilæ*, and rather to reason than to drink profoundly. But in this innocent intention they were interrupted by the disturbance arising from a little quarrel, in which some of the ruder people in the house were for a short time engaged. At this Mr. Hobbes seemed much concerned, though he was at some distance from the persons." And why was he concerned, gentlemen? No doubt you fancy, from some benign and disinterested love of peace and harmony, worthy of an old man and a philosopher. But listen,—"For a while he was not composed, but related it once or twice as to himself, with a low and careful tone, how Sextus Roscius was murthered after supper by the Balneæ Palatinæ. Of such general extent is that remark of Cicero, in relation to Epicurus the Atheist, of whom he observed that he of all men dreaded most those things which he contemned,—Death and the Gods." Merely because it was supper-time, and in the neighborhood of a bath, Mr. Hobbes must have the fate of Sextus Roscius. What logic was there in this, unless to a man who was always dreaming of murder? Here was Leviathan, no longer afraid of the daggers of English cavaliers or French clergy, but "frightened from his propriety" by a row in an alehouse between some honest clodhoppers of Derbyshire, whom his own gaunt scarecrow of a person, that belonged to quite another century, would have frightened out of their wits.

Malebranche, it will give you pleasure to hear, was murdered. The man who murdered him is well known; it was Bishop Berkeley. The story is familiar, though hitherto not put in a proper light. Berkeley, when a young man, went to Paris and called on Père Malebranche. He found him in his cell cooking. Cooks have ever been a *genus irritabile*; authors still more so; Malebranche was both; a dispute arose; the old father, warm already, became warmer; culinary and metaphysical irritations united to derange his liver: he took to his bed, and died. Such is the common version of the story: "So the whole ear of Denmark is abused." The fact is, that the matter was hushed up, out of consideration for Berkeley, who (as Pope remarked) had "every virtue under heaven": else it was well known that Berkeley, feeling himself nettled by the waspishness of the old Frenchman, squared at him; a *turn-up* was the consequence; Malebranche was floored in the first round; the conceit was wholly taken out of him; and he would perhaps have given in; but Berkeley's blood was now up, and he insisted on the old Frenchman's retracting his doctrine of Occasional Causes. The vanity of the man was too great for this; and he fell a sacrifice to the impetuosity of Irish youth, combined with his own absurd obstinacy.

Leibnitz being every way superior to Malebranche, one might, *a fortiori*, have counted on *his* being murdered; which, however, was not the case. I believe he was nettled at this neglect, and felt himself insulted by the security in which he passed his days. In no other way can I explain his conduct at the latter end of his life, when he chose to grow very avaricious, and to hoard up large sums of gold, which he kept in his own house. This was at Vienna, where he died; and letters are still in existence, describing the immeasurable anxiety which he entertained for his throat. Still his ambition, for being *attempted* at least, was so great, that he would not forego the danger. A late English pedagogue, of Birmingham manufacture, namely, Dr. Parr, took a more selfish course, under the same circumstances. He had amassed a considerable quantity of gold and silver plate, which was for some time deposited in his bedroom at his parsonage house, Hatton. But growing every day more afraid of being murdered, which he knew that he could not stand, and to which, indeed, he never had the slightest pretension, he transferred the whole to the Hatton blacksmith; conceiving, no doubt, that the murder of a blacksmith would fall more lightly on the *salus reipublicæ* than that of a pedagogue. But I have heard this greatly disputed; and it seems now generally agreed that one good horseshoe is worth about two and one fourth Spital sermons.

As Leibnitz, though not murdered, may be said to have died, partly of the fear that he should be murdered, and partly of vexation that he was not,— Kant, on the other hand, who had no ambition in that way, had a narrower escape from a murderer than any man we read of, except Des Cartes. So absurdly does Fortune throw about her favors! The case is told, I think, in an anonymous life of this very great man. For health's sake, Kant imposed upon himself, at one time, a walk of six miles every day along a high-road. This fact becoming known to a man who had his private reasons for committing murder, at the third milestone from Konigsberg, he waited for his "intended," who came up to time as duly as a mail-coach.

But for an accident, Kant was a dead man. However, on considerations of "morality," it happened that the murderer preferred a little child, whom he saw playing in the road, to the old transcendentalist: this child he murdered; and thus it happened that Kant escaped. Such is the German account of the matter; but my opinion is, that the murderer was an amateur, who felt how little would be gained to the cause of good taste by murdering an old, arid, and adust metaphysician; there was no room for display, as the man could not possibly look more like a mummy when dead than he had done alive.

———

Thus, gentlemen, I have traced the connection between philosophy and our art, until insensibly I find that I have wandered into our own era. This I shall not take any pains to characterize apart from that which preceded it, for, in fact, they have no distinct character. The seventeenth and eighteenth centuries, together with so much of the nineteenth as we have yet seen, jointly compose the Augustan age of murder. The finest work of the seventeenth century is, unquestionably, the murder of Sir Edmondbury Godfrey, which has my entire approbation. At the same time, it must be observed that the quantity of murder was not great in this century, at least amongst our own artists; which, perhaps, is attributable to the want of enlightened patronage. *Sint Mæcenates, non deerunt, Flacce, Marones.* Consulting Grant's "Observations on the Bills of Mortality" (4th edition, Oxford, 1665), I find that, out of 229,250, who died in London during one period of twenty years, in the seventeenth century, not more than eighty-six were murdered; that is, about four and three tenths per annum. A small number this, gentlemen, to found an academy upon; and certainly, where the quantity is so small, we have a right to expect that the quality should be first-rate. Perhaps it was; yet still I am of opinion that the best artist in this century was not equal to the best in that which followed. For instance, however praiseworthy the case of Sir Edmondbury Godfrey may be (and nobody can be more sensible of its merits than I am), still, I cannot consent to place it on a level with that of Mrs. Ruscombe of Bristol, either as to originality of design, or boldness and breadth of style. This good lady's murder took place early in the reign of George III., a reign which was notoriously favorable to the arts generally. She lived in College Green, with a single maid-servant, neither of them having any pretension to the notice of history but what they derived from the great artist whose workmanship I am recording. One fine morning, when all Bristol was alive and in motion, some suspicion arising, the neighbors forced an entrance into the house, and found Mrs. Ruscombe murdered in her bedroom, and the servant murdered on the stairs: this was at noon; and, not more than two hours before, both mistress and servant had been seen alive. To the best of my remembrance, this was in 1764; upwards of sixty years, therefore, have now elapsed, and yet the artist is still undiscovered. The suspicions of posterity have settled upon two pretenders,—a baker and a chimney-sweeper. But posterity is wrong; no unpractised artist could have conceived so bold an idea as that of a noonday murder in the heart of a great city. It was no obscure baker, gentlemen, or anonymous chimney-sweeper, be assured, that executed this work. I know who it was. (*Here there was a general buzz, which at length broke out into open applause; upon which the lecturer blushed, and went on with much earnestness.*) For Heaven's sake, gentlemen, do not mistake me; it was not I that did it. I have not the vanity to think myself equal to any such achievement; be assured that you greatly overrate my poor talents; Mrs. Ruscombe's affair was far beyond my slender abilities. But I came to know who the artist was, from a celebrated surgeon, who assisted at his dissection. This gentleman had a private museum in the way of his profession, one corner of which was occupied by a cast from a man of remarkably fine proportions.

"That," said the surgeon, "is a cast from the celebrated Lancashire highwayman, who concealed his profession for some time from his neighbors, by drawing woollen stockings over his horse's legs, and in that way muffling the clatter which he must else have made in riding up a flagged alley that led to his stable. At the time of his execution for highway robbery, I was studying under Cruickshank; and the man's figure was so uncommonly fine, that no money or exertion was spared to get into possession of him with the least possible delay. By the connivance of the under-sheriff, he was cut down within the legal time, and instantly put into a chaise and four; so that, when he reached Cruickshank's he was positively not dead. Mr.——, a young student at that time, had the honor of giving him the *coup de grace*, and finishing the sentence of the law." This remarkable anecdote, which seemed to imply that all the gentlemen in the dissecting-room were amateurs of our class, struck me a good deal; and I was repeating it one day to a Lancashire lady, who thereupon informed me that she had herself lived in the neighborhood of that highwayman, and well remembered two circumstances, which combined, in the opinion of all his neighbors, to fix upon him the credit of Mrs. Ruscombe's affair. One was, the fact of his absence for a whole fortnight at the period of that murder; the other that, within a very little time after, the neighborhood of this highwayman was deluged with dollars: now Mrs. Ruscombe was known to have hoarded about two thousand of that coin. Be the artist, however, who he might, the affair remains a durable monument of his genius; for such was the impression of awe, and the sense of power left behind, by the strength of conception manifested in this murder, that no tenant (as I was told in 1810) had been found up to that time for Mrs. Ruscombe's house.

But, whilst I thus eulogize the Ruscombian case, let me not be supposed to overlook the many other specimens of extraordinary merit spread over the face of this century. Such cases, indeed, as that of Miss Bland, or of Captain Donnellan, and Sir Theophilus Boughton, shall never have any countenance from me. Fie on these dealers in poison, say I; can they not keep to the old honest way of cutting throats, without introducing such abominable innovations from Italy? I consider all these poisoning cases, compared with the legitimate style, as no better than waxwork by the side of sculpture, or a lithographic print by the side of a fine Volpato. But, dismissing these, there remain many excellent works of art in a pure style, such as nobody need be ashamed to own, as every candid connoisseur will admit. *Candid*, observe, I say; for great allowances must be made in these cases; no artist can ever be sure of carrying through his own fine preconception. Awkward disturbances will arise: people will not submit to have their throats cut quietly; they will run, they will kick, they will bite; and whilst the portrait-painter often has to complain of too much torpor in his subject, the artist in our line is generally embarrassed by too much animation. At the same time, however disagreeable to the artist, this tendency in murder to excite and irritate the subject is certainly one of its advantages to the world in general, which we ought not to overlook, since it favors the development of latent talent. Jeremy Taylor notices, with admiration, the extraordinary leaps which people will take under the influence of fear. There was a striking instance of this in the recent case of the M'Keands; the boy cleared a height such as he will never clear again to his dying day. Talents also of the most brilliant description for thumping, and indeed for all the gymnastic exercises, have sometimes been developed by the panic which accompanies our artists; talents else buried and hid under a bushel to the possessors, as much as to their friends. I remember an interesting illustration of this fact, in a case which I learned in Germany.

Riding one day in the neighborhood of Munich, I overtook a distinguished amateur of our society, whose name I shall conceal. This gentleman informed me that, finding himself wearied with the frigid pleasures (so he called them) of mere amateurship, he had quitted England for the continent,—meaning to practise a little professionally. For this purpose he resorted to Germany, conceiving the police in that part of Europe to be more heavy and drowsy than elsewhere. His *début*, as a practitioner, took place at Mannheim; and, knowing me to be a brother amateur, he freely communicated the whole of his maiden adventure. "Opposite to my lodging," said he, "lived a baker: he was somewhat of a miser, and lived quite alone. Whether it were his great expanse of chalky face, or what else, I know not, but the fact was, I 'fancied' him, and resolved to commence business upon his throat, which, by the way, he always carried bare,—a fashion which is very irritating to my desires. Precisely at eight o'clock in the evening, I observed that he regularly shut up his windows. One night I watched him when thus engaged,—bolted in after him,—locked the door,—and, addressing him with great suavity, acquainted him with the nature of my errand; at the same time advising him to make no resistance, which would be mutually unpleasant. So saying, I drew out my tools, and was proceeding to operate. But at this spectacle, the baker, who seemed to have been struck by catalepsy at my first announce, awoke into tremendous agitation. 'I will *not* be murdered!' he shrieked aloud; 'what for will I lose my precious throat?' 'What for?' said I; 'if for no other reason, for this,—that you put alum into your bread. But no matter, alum or no alum (for I was resolved to forestall any argument on that point), know that I am a virtuoso in the art of murder, am desirous of improving myself in its details, and am enamored of your vast surface of throat, to which I am determined to be a customer.' 'Is it so?' said he, 'but I'll find you a customer in another line.' And so saying, he threw himself into a boxing attitude. The very idea of his boxing struck me as ludicrous. It is true, a London baker had distinguished himself in the ring, and became known to fame under the title of the Master of the Rolls; but he was young and unspoiled; whereas, this man was a monstrous feather-bed in person, fifty years old, and totally out of condition. Spite of all this, however, and contending against me, who am a master in the art, he made so desperate a defence that many times I feared he might turn the tables upon me; and that I, an amateur, might be murdered by a rascally baker. What a situation! Minds of sensibility will sympathize with my anxiety. How severe it was, you may understand by this that for the first thirteen rounds the baker had the advantage. Round the fourteenth, I received a blow on the right eye, which closed it up; in the end, I believe, this was my salvation; for the anger it roused in me was so great that, in this and every one of the three following rounds, I floored the baker.

"Round 18th. The baker came up piping, and manifestly the worse for wear. His geometrical exploits in the four last rounds had done him no good. However, he showed some skill in stopping a message which I was sending to his cadaverous mug: in delivering which, my foot slipped, and I went down.

"Round 19th. Surveying the baker, I became ashamed of having been so much bothered by a shapeless mass of dough; and I went in fiercely, and administered some severe punishment. A rally took place,—both went down,—baker undermost,—ten to three on amateur.

"Round 20th. The baker jumped up with surprising agility: indeed, he managed his pins capitally, and fought wonderfully, considering that he was drenched in perspiration; but the shine was now taken out of him, and his game was the mere effect of panic. It was now clear that he could not last much longer. In the course of this round we tried the weaving system, in which I had greatly the advantage, and hit him repeatedly on the conk. My reason for this was, that his conk was covered with carbuncles; and I thought I should vex him by taking such liberties with his conk, which in fact I did.

"The three next rounds, the master of the rolls staggered about like a cow on the ice. Seeing how matters stood, in round twenty-fourth I whispered something into his ear, which sent him down like a shot. It was nothing more than my private opinion of the value of his throat at an annuity office. This little confidential whisker affected him greatly; the very perspiration was frozen on his face, and for the next two rounds I had it all my own way. And when I called *time* for the twenty-seventh round, he lay like a log on the floor."

"After which," said I to the amateur, "it may be presumed that you accomplished your purpose." "You are right," said he, mildly, "I did; and a great satisfaction, you know, it was to my mind, for by this means I killed two birds with one stone"; meaning that he had both thumped the baker and murdered him. Now, for the life of me, I could not see *that*; for, on the contrary, to my mind it appeared that he had taken two stones to kill one bird, having been obliged to take the conceit out of him first with his fist, and then with his tools. But no matter for his logic. The moral of his story was good, for it showed what an astonishing stimulus to latent talent is contained in any reasonable prospect of being murdered. A pursy, unwieldy, half-cataleptic baker of Mannheim had absolutely fought six-and-twenty rounds with an accomplished English boxer merely upon this inspiration; so greatly was natural genius exalted and sublimed by the genial presence of his murderer.

Really, gentlemen, when one hears of such things as these, it becomes a duty, perhaps, a little to soften that extreme asperity with which most men speak of murder. To hear people talk, you would suppose that all the disadvantages and inconveniences were on the side of being murdered, and that there were none at all in *not* being murdered. But considerate men think otherwise. "Certainly," says Jeremy Taylor, "it is a less temporal evil to fall by the rudeness of a sword than the violence of a fever; and the axe" (to which he might have added the ship-carpenter's mallet and the crowbar) "is a much less affliction than a strangury." Very true; the bishop talks like a wise man and an amateur, as he is; and another great philosopher, Marcus Aurelius, was equally above the vulgar prejudices on this subject. He declares it to be one of "the noblest functions of reason to know whether it is time to walk out of the world or not." (Book III., Collers's Translation.) No sort of knowledge being rarer than this, surely *that* man must be a most philanthropic character, who undertakes to instruct people in this branch of knowledge gratis, and at no little hazard to himself. All this, however, I throw out only in the way of speculation to future moralists; declaring in the mean time my own private conviction, that very few men commit murder upon philanthropic or patriotic principles, and repeating what I have already said once at least,—that, as to the majority of murderers, they are very incorrect characters.

With respect to Williams's murders, the sublimest and most entire in their excellence that ever were committed, I shall not allow myself to speak incidentally. Nothing less than an entire lecture, or even an entire course of lectures, would suffice to expound their merits. But one curious fact, connected with his case, I shall mention, because it seems to imply that the blaze of his genius absolutely dazzled the eye of criminal justice. You all remember, I doubt not, that the instruments with which he executed his first great work (the murder of the Marrs) were a ship-carpenter's mallet and a knife. Now, the mallet belonged to an old Swede, one John Peterson, and bore his initials. This instrument Williams left behind him, in Marr's house, and it fell into the hands of the magistrates. Now, gentlemen, it is a fact that the publication of this circumstance of the initials led immediately to the apprehension of Williams, and, if made earlier, would have prevented his second great work, the murder of the Williamsons, which took place precisely twelve days after. But the magistrates kept back this fact from the public for the entire twelve days, and until that second work was accomplished. That finished, they published it, apparently feeling that Williams had now done enough for his fame, and that his glory was at length placed beyond the reach of accident.

As to Mr. Thurtell's case, I know not what to say. Naturally, I have every disposition to think highly of my predecessor in the chair of this society; and I acknowledge that his lectures were unexceptionable. But, speaking ingenuously, I do really think that his principal performance, as an artist, has been much overrated. I admit that at first I was myself carried away by the general enthusiasm. On the morning when the murder was made known in London, there was the fullest meeting of amateurs that I have ever known since the days of Williams; old bedridden connoisseurs, who had got into a peevish way of sneering and complaining "that there was nothing doing," now hobbled down to our clubroom: such hilarity, such benign expression of general satisfaction, I have rarely witnessed. On every side you saw people shaking hands, congratulating each other, and forming dinner-parties for the evening; and nothing was to be heard but triumphant challenges of, "Well! will *this* do?" "Is *this* the right thing?" "Are you satisfied at last?" But, in the midst of this, I remember we all grew silent on hearing the old cynical amateur, L. S———, that *laudator temporis acti*, stumping along with his wooden leg; he entered the room with his usual scowl, and, as he advanced, he continued to growl and stutter the whole way. "Not an original idea in the whole piece,—mere plagiarism,—base plagiarism from hints that I threw out! Besides, his style is as hard as Albert Durer, and as coarse as Fuseli." Many thought that this was mere jealousy and general waspishness; but I confess that when the first glow of enthusiasm had subsided, I have found most judicious critics to agree that there was something *falsetto* in the style of Thurtell. The fact is, he was a member of our society, which naturally gave a friendly bias to our judgments; and his person was universally familiar to the cockneys, which gave him, with the whole London public, a temporary popularity, that his pretensions are not capable of supporting; for *opinionum commenta delet dies, naturæ judicia confirmat*. There was, however, an unfinished design of Thurtell's for the murder of a man with a pair of dumbbells, which I admired greatly; it was a mere outline, that he never completed; but to my mind it seemed every way superior to his chief work. I remember that there was great regret expressed by some amateurs that this sketch should have been left in an unfinished state: but there I cannot agree with them; for the fragments and first bold outlines of original artists have often a felicity about them which is apt to vanish in the management of the details.

The case of the M'Keands I consider far beyond the vaunted performance of Thurtell,—indeed, above all praise; and bearing that relation, in fact, to the immortal works of Williams which the Æneid bears to the Iliad.

But it is now time that I should say a few words about the principles of murder, not with a view to regulate your practice, but your judgment: as to old women, and the mob of newspaper readers, they are pleased with anything, provided it is bloody enough. But the mind of sensibility requires something more. *First*, then, let us speak of the kind of person who is adapted to the purpose of the murderer; *secondly*, of the place where; *thirdly*, of the time when, and other little circumstances.

As to the person, I suppose it is evident that he ought to be a good man; because, if he were not, he might himself, by possibility, be contemplating murder at the very time; and such "diamond-cut-diamond" tussles, though pleasant enough where nothing better is stirring, are really not what a critic can allow himself to call murders. I could mention some people (I name no names) who have been murdered by other people in a dark lane; and so far all seemed correct enough; but, on looking further into the matter, the public have become aware that the murdered party was himself, at the moment, planning to rob his murderer, at the least, and possibly to murder him, if he had been strong enough. Whenever that is the case, or may be thought to be the case, farewell to all the genuine effects of the art. For the final purpose of murder, considered as a fine art, is precisely the same as that of tragedy, in Aristotle's account of it, namely, "to cleanse the heart by means of pity and terror." Now, terror there may be, but how can there be any pity for one tiger destroyed by another tiger?

It is also evident that the person selected ought not to be a public character. For instance, no judicious artist would have attempted to murder Abraham Newland. For the case was this: everybody read so much about Abraham Newland, and so few people ever saw him, that there was a fixed belief that he was an abstract idea. And I remember that once, when I happened to mention that I had dined at a coffee-house in company with Abraham Newland, everybody looked scornfully at me, as though I had pretended to have played at billiards with Prester John, or to have had an affair of honor with the Pope. And, by the way, the Pope would be a very improper person to murder: for he has such a virtual ubiquity as the father of Christendom, and, like the cuckoo, is so often heard but never seen, that I suspect most people regard *him* also as an abstract idea. Where, indeed, a public character is in the habit of giving dinners, "with every delicacy of the season," the case is very different: every person is satisfied that *he* is no abstract idea; and, therefore, there can be no impropriety in murdering him; only that his murder will fall into the class of assassinations, which I have not yet treated.

Thirdly. The subject chosen ought to be in good health; for it is absolutely barbarous to murder a sick person, who is usually quite unable to bear it. On this principle, no cockney ought to be chosen who is above twenty-five, for after that age he is sure to be dyspeptic. Or at least, if a man will hunt in that warren, he ought to murder a couple at one time; if the cockneys chosen should be tailors, he will of course think it his duty, on the old-established equation, to murder eighteen. And, here, in this attention to the comfort of sick people, you will observe the usual effect of a fine art to soften and refine the feelings. The world in general, gentlemen, are very bloody-minded; and all they want in a murder is a copious effusion of blood; gaudy display in this point is enough for *them*. But the enlightened connoisseur is more refined in his taste; and from our art, as from all the other liberal arts when thoroughly cultivated, the result is, to improve and to humanize the heart; so true is it, that

"Ingenuas didicisse fideliter artes,
Emollit mores, nec sinit esse feros."

A philosophic friend, well known for his philanthropy and general benignity, suggests that the subject chosen ought also to have a family of young children wholly dependent on his exertions, by way of deepening the pathos. And, undoubtedly, this is a judicious caution. Yet I would not insist too keenly on this condition. Severe good taste unquestionably demands it; but still, where the man was otherwise unobjectionable in point of morals and health, I would not look with too curious a jealousy to a restriction which might have the effect of narrowing the artist's sphere.

So much for the person. As to the time, the place, and the tools, I have many things to say, which at present I have no room for. The good sense of the practitioner has usually directed him to night and privacy. Yet there have not been wanting cases where this rule was departed from with excellent effect. In respect to time, Mrs. Ruscombe's case is a beautiful exception, which I have already noticed; and in respect both to time and place, there is a fine exception in the annals of Edinburgh (year 1805), familiar to every child in Edinburgh, but which has unaccountably been defrauded of its due portion of fame amongst English amateurs. The case I mean is that of a porter to one of the banks, who was murdered whilst carrying a bag of money, in broad daylight, on turning out of the High Street, one of the most public streets in Europe, and the murderer is to this hour undiscovered.

"Sed fugit interea, fugit irreparabile tempus,
Singula dum capti circumvectamur amore."

And now, gentlemen, in conclusion, let me again solemnly disclaim all pretensions on my own part to the character of a professional man. I never attempted any murder in my life, except in the year 1801, upon the body of a tom-cat; and *that* turned out differently from my intention. My purpose, I own, was downright murder. "Semper ego auditor tantum?" said I, "nunquamne reponam?" And I went down stairs in search of Tom at one o'clock on a dark night, with the "animus" and no doubt with the fiendish looks of a murderer. But when I found him, he was in the act of plundering the pantry of bread and other things. Now this gave a new turn to the affair; for the time being one of general scarcity, when even Christians were reduced to the use of potato-bread, rice-bread, and all sorts of things, it was downright treason in a tom-cat to be wasting good wheaten-bread in the way he was doing. It instantly became a patriotic duty to put him to death; and as I raised aloft and shook the glittering steel, I fancied myself rising like Brutus, effulgent from a crowd of patriots, and, as I stabbed him, I

"Called aloud on Tully's name,
And bade the father of his country hail!"

Since then, what wandering thoughts I may have had of attempting the life of an ancient ewe, of a superannuated hen, and such "small deer," are locked up in the secrets of my own breast; but for the higher departments of the art, I confess myself to be utterly unfit. My ambition does not rise so high. No, gentlemen, in the words of Horace,—

"Fungar vice cotis, acutum
Reddere quæ ferrum valet, exsors ipsa secandi."

THE CAPTAIN'S STORY.
BY REBECCA HARDING DAVIS.

I HAVE been asked to tell what I know of the case of Joseph C. Wylie, whose mysterious disappearance caused so much excitement in Cincinnati when it occurred. That was in '58, however, before the war; and I had supposed all trace of the affair had been swept from the public mind by the events which followed. Indeed, I see no reason for reviving it now, except that it bears more fully than any evidence I have ever heard upon the curious matter called spiritualism, and I have thought (though I am only a plain man, not used to dealing in such whimseys) it offers a key to unlock the riddle.

Wylie was a river-hand; ran the Ohio and Lower Mississippi as clerk and captain on several stern-wheelers, so came to be known pretty generally along shore. He was with me as second clerk when the thing happened. I was running the Jacob Strader, one of the largest steamboats on the Mississippi. I took little account of the fellow; he was a small, red-headed, weak-eyed man, shambling lazily about, whose legs and arms seemed scarcely to have gristle enough in them to hold them firmly together.

The only noteworthy trait about him was that he never touched liquor or a card, but found his amusement, instead, in sitting with some of the deck hands below, telling long pointless yarns. I had to stop it at last. That runs contrary to my notions of discipline.

It was in April that he disappeared, like a flea, under my very eyes. The Strader lay at the wharf, at Cincinnati; it was Sunday, about noon; she was to get up steam at seven o'clock next morning. I walked up the levee, and just off the cobble-stones met Wylie. He had a drum of figs in his hand which he had just bought from some pedler on the David Swan, and was going to take home to his little Joe, in Cairo, he said, as he walked alongside of me.

I met John Fordyce, and stopped to get a light of him; Wylie went into a shanty fitted up as a shop for the sale of cigars, newspapers, and the like; he wanted a "Despatch," he said. The shop was but a single room, opening, front and back, on the wide (and at that hour on Sunday morning), empty wharf; a square, plank-built affair, made to hold the two counters and a stove in the middle. Wylie went into it, as I said, but out of it he was never seen to come alive. I stood talking with Fordyce for some minutes, then called the clerk, and when he did not answer, went in search of him, but found only the boy who tended the shop, asleep under the counter. Wylie was not there, nor on the boat, nor on the wharf. He was nowhere, so far as the sharpest eyes of the Cincinnati police could discover.

The thing staggered me when I had time to take it home and realize that the man was actually gone; spirited away in broad daylight, before my face. It was absurd, impossible; yet it struck me with a sort of horror that did not belong to midnight murder.

They called it murder in the papers; there was a great outcry; but where was the foul play? The boy (a child of ten) had heard or seen nothing; it was impossible that Wylie could have been foully dealt with, and no sound or cry reach Fordyce or me, half a dozen feet off. It was just as impossible that he could have left the shop, unseen by us on the wide, open levee. That he could have gone voluntarily, nobody hinted. The poor fellow had but few ideas beyond his wife and boy, Joe. His trunk on board was found filled with cheap summer clothes for them both, some tinware, a japanned tea-tray, a china mug; trifles which he had gathered up at auctions, and was taking to Cairo to make their little home comfortable. He had made an engagement to go out with the first clerk that afternoon; his clean shirt, collar, and shaving apparatus were all laid out in his state-room.

But that was the last of him. It only remained to gather up these things and carry them with the news to his wife.

I shirked that. I cannot face a woman in trouble. I ordered Stein, who had been a sort of crony of his, to do it. Stein was the steward, and was leaving the boat. He had a good berth offered to him in St. Louis, he said; so that I knew he had time to see Wylie's widow, and break it gently to her.

If widow she was. If Wylie had died naturally I would have dismissed him from my mind; but the matter rankled there, as I might say, from its very doubt and mystery.

About two years afterward, therefore, when Warrick brought a little boy on board, as the boat lay at Cairo, and told me it was Wylie's son, I found myself going, again and again, to the part of the deck where the child was playing, feeling pained to notice how coarsely dressed it was, and how pinched, even hunger-bitten, the little honest face.

"Is it going so badly with her?" I asked.

Warrick nodded, saying aloud, "Joe's shaken with the whooping-cough, Captain. He's the deuce of a boy for sniffing up all the ailments that are going up and down the river."

Joe looked up and laughed.

"He had better shake them down into the river again, then," I said. "Let him and his mother come aboard for a trip or two. Nothing like air off of water for that whoop, the old women say."

I sent Warrick to urge the plan on Mrs. Wylie. I knew it was not the air that was needed so much as good, wholesome food. Warrick set apart the best state-room for her, and I dropped in myself to see that it was all in order.

In the evening, before we started, Warrick brought her aboard and into the cabin where I was. I found that she had some exaggerated notions about one or two good turns I had done her husband, and a trifle which I had sent to her when he was lost; so, after that, I held aloof from her. I hate philandering. I kept an eye, though, to see how she fared,—on the little body in her rusty black gown, shying round with Joe in the corners, out of the way of the ladies who went sweeping their long dresses up and down.

I soon found, however, that all the men on board who had known Wylie, from Warrick down, vied with each other in treating her with a sort of patronizing respect; even Jake, the black cook, was continually sending up little messes for her and Joe. She was but a poor mouse of a woman, who had made a god of that stupid little weak-eyed fellow, and of his boy after he was gone; take her on politics, or even gossip, anything outside of Wylie and her child, and there was nothing in her. Warrick told me that she had never been outside of Cairo before, and the near village of Blandville, where she had been a sempstress before her marriage; this journey was like a glimpse of a new world to her. I used to see her sitting in a dark corner on deck until late in the night, her eyes strained over the long stretch of shore as we floated by; and I could understand how the heavy, wooded hills, crouching like sullen beasts along the water's edge, or the miles and miles of yellow cane-brake lying flat and barren in the desolate, homesick twilight of a winter's day, might have a different meaning to the lonely woman, and to us, who counted them only as "a run" of so many hours.

She was sitting this way one evening on our back trip, when the boat stopped to wood at a place called by the boatmen Dead Man's Riffle. Warrick was near me, watching her.

"She wears black," he said, at last. "Now for me," cutting off a quid of tobacco, "I never believed Joe Wylie was dead. No, it was a bad bit of work, dead or alive,—bad."

"It is work I would give much to see cleared up, before I die," I said. Warrick and I were walking up and down the hurricane-deck.

"Would you?" he said, slowly, chewing and glancing up at me,—"would you? There's a way. But no matter—" stopping short and looking ashamed.

I said nothing. I never urge a man to speak, if he has ever so little mind to hold his tongue quiet. But Warrick had some notion that troubled him. He walked nearer at each turn to the place where a stout, short young woman was sitting, dressed in brown linsey. There was nothing remarkable about her face, which was heavy and dull, if we except a pair of thick, dead, fishy gray eyes.

"Do you see that girl?" he jerked out. "Many of the men aboard would say that she could tell you anything you want to know; the dead are about her all the time, they say. *I* don't say it, Captain, mind; I'm not such a fool."

"I should hope not, Warrick," I said, gravely, and began to talk of something else. But somehow the matter stuck in my mind. The next day we stopped for freight at Natchez. I went up into the city with one of the passengers. Old Jimmy A. it was,—anybody on the Western waters will know who I mean; for strangers I will only say that A. was one of the most thorough misers I ever knew. He was an extensive stock-broker and speculator in Western lands. When his wife lived he had always consulted her, and abode by her advice in his business. I believe he mourned for the old woman sincerely, though when she died he had taken the ribbon away with which the women had bound her chin and put twine instead, to save a penny.

A. was my companion, as I said. Coming down into the old town a sudden idea struck me.

"These lots are cheap, Mr. A.," I said. "Buy them and put up good dwellings on them, and your fortune is made. Real estate is going up here daily."

The old man seized on the plan eagerly, and held me by the coat while he went about the lots, calculating, muttering, chuckling to himself.

"It's a good notion, very good. This swamp could be drained,—it would bring in eleven per cent, eleven and a half—and a half; I wish I knew what Ann would think of it, poor Ann! I've a great mind to go into it; I have indeed."

It was with difficulty I got the old fellow away and on board in time before the boat put off. It was growing dusk as we stepped off the plank on deck. A. still clung to me, following me up and down, charging me to say nothing of the plan until he had well considered it. As we went up to the outer cabin we met the woman to whom Warrick had directed my notice the day before. She was pacing up and down with heavy, masculine steps; she stood still as we came up; her dead gray eyes fell on A. and rested there with a curious absorbing look; which, perhaps, I should not have seen but for Warrick's warning.

She remained quite quiet until we had passed and returned; then stooping suddenly to a table before her, wrote on a scrap of paper, and handed it to the old man, walking away after she had done so; every motion lifeless, mechanical, like a clumsy machine of wood set in action.

A. had not seen her, I think, until she thrust the paper into his hand; he stared, pulled at his ragged gray beard, and then peered at it through his spectacles. There was a queer, scared little noise in his throat, like the crow of a chicken.

"Why, Captain, look here! this is—is—" holding out the dirty scrap of paper.

It was a message from his wife. "Do not touch real estate, except to mortgage," she said. "The drainage of the swamp would eat up four years' profits."

("I thought of that," he interrupted, quickly.) "Do not withdraw your money from P. C."

"That is all," I said. "Who is this woman, Mr. A.?"

"God knows. But no human being alive knew of that P. C. money. *Ann did.*" His face was colorless and his teeth chattered. We went to the woman. She was apparently stolid, and but half educated; I saw no sign of cunning, even shrewdness, about her.

"The message had been given to her," she said. "How, she did not know."

"From a spirit?"

"She could not say that. She supposed so. They called her a writing medium."

Afterward she said, "This thing would ruin her," crying in a feeble, stupid way. She had been an operative in some mill in Cincinnati, we were told, and was discharged in consequence of it. The "manifestations" were followed by attacks of something resembling paralysis, which would soon leave her helpless. I left the old man talking to her.

Warrick came to me that evening. He had heard of the affair. "Captain," he said, "I'm going to try if no tidings can be had from Joe Wylie. Have I your permission?" I nodded, shortly. Warrick's broad face was pale and anxious. I sat for a while looking at the closed door of the little office into which they had gone. Then I got up and followed them. The woman (Lusk was her name) was there, Warrick, and the wife of the carpenter,—a shrewd, sensible woman,—who had been a friend of Wylie's, as most women were.

She and the girl sat facing each other at a table on which flared a dirty oil lamp. Warrick leaned on the back of a chair with both hands, watching the girl's face.

"She knows what she's got to do, Captain," vigorously chewing and spitting, but not lifting his eyes. "I told her to consult her familiar spirit, or whatever it is. Let's have him up! Let's know what's become of Joe, good or bad."

I had seen Warrick cool and grave when a burning boat was drifting with all aboard right into the rapids; but now he was a coward in every bone of his body; his very voice grew piping and boisterous as the woman turned her square, heavy face toward him, and the gray eyes, which they said saw the dead, fell on his.

For the girl, I observed that she had the appearance of extreme nervous dejection; her breath was uncertain and feeble; her lips blue. I touched her and found that the blood had almost ceased to circulate. Her temples were hot; hands icy cold; the pupils of the eyes contracted. The look was *fastened into* Warrick. I can describe it in no other way. I shook her, but could not loosen the hold of it. It was as if she drew the life out of his burly big body with her dull eyes.

"Bring up the spirit of Wylie, my woman," he said, with a loud, uneasy laugh that suddenly died into profound silence.

She shook her head; raised her forefinger slowly, pointing into the shadow behind him.

"What do you see?"

"I see a ship—three-masted—a bark." (Warrick started, nodding his head with a muttered oath.) "The sea is frozen; the ship is wedged between masses of ice; the sky is like a bronze plane above; there is neither sun nor wind."

"On a whaler!" burst in Warrick. "I always knew it! I was in just such a scrape, off—Go on, go on."

"There are two men on deck. One is heavily built, gray-headed; the other is spare, short, with red hair. There is a blood-mark on his chin."

"Wylie! Alive!"

"Alive. His clothes are gray—"

"He wore gray the day he left," said Warrick. "But, come to think of it now, he wouldn't—"

"I was wrong. He wears a sailor's dress."

She got up hastily, putting her hand to her forehead. Her face was covered with a cold sweat. "Nothing—nothing! I am sick. Stop—no more," she gasped.

Mrs. Pallet, the carpenter's wife, put her arm about her. "I'll take her to her room, Captain?" looking at me. "There's no cheating in her, at any rate," as she led her out. "It's my belief it's the Devil's work."

Warrick straightened himself and drew a long breath. "Do you think it is the Devil's work, sir?"

"God knows."

"It is the truth, whether or no. Wylie always had a hankering for a sea life. He used to listen to my old whaling yarns twenty times over. And I've heard lately, Captain, that poor Joe was deep in debt when he disappeared. Some old matters, before he came aboard the Strader. He had a reason for going. But Ellen thinks him dead,—thinks him dead," stroking his whiskers. "Would you tell her of this now, eh, Captain?" looking up.

"Yes, I would," after a pause. "It can do no harm. But gently, Warrick, gently."

It did do harm, however gently it was told. The next day Wylie's wife came to me where I stood alone, near the texas. Her nose was red from crying, and her eyes angry, which made the rest of her face more hunger-nipped and pale. She touched my sleeve, and then drew off, holding her little boy by the hand.

"Captain Roberts," she said, in a low, steady voice, "there is a woman on the boat who pretends to have seen my husband alive. If he is alive, he has deserted me. He is dead."

"Be calm, madam."

"He is dead. You shall not think ill of Joe." She was silent a moment, holding her throat with one hand. "If he is alive, he has deserted me, and— I'll tell you, Captain Roberts, but I never meant to tell any living man. When you brought me and Joe on the boat, I hadn't touched meat for four months. It took all I could make to keep life in the boy, and barely that. I went out scrubbing when sewing failed me. I scrubbed and whitewashed. I didn't beg. Do you think Joe would have left me to that? and him alive? He's dead. There's some days I've went through—if Joe had been on the face of the earth he'd have come to me them days. He's dead; he's waiting, somewheres—"

She held little Joe tighter by the hand, looking beyond me—God knows where—into the place where old Joe waited for her, I suppose; the somewheres where the poor starved soul hoped to find the comfort and love of her married life again. I hesitated. "Would you like to see this woman? I will not say that I credit her assertions, but there is a curious—"

She drew herself up, growing pale. "I, sir? No; I only wished that you should do my husband justice. For the woman—no matter. I will not detain you, Captain Roberts." And so, scarcely waiting for me to speak to the boy, she drew him away with her.

"That cut Ellen hard," Warrick said,—"hard. These women would rather a man should die any day than cease to care for them. But it's true. Joe Wylie went on a whaler, sir."

The girl Lusk went ashore at New Albany, and I saw her no more. She became afterward a noted medium, I believe; and old A., by the way, used to consult her in all of his undertakings, or rather his wife, through her.

The matter puzzled me. I did *not* believe the spirits of the dead had anything to do with it; though the woman, before she went off the boat, brought me a message from one who has been gone from me this many a year. I will say no more of this. Since she died I have not named her name. I did not believe the words came from her. I did not believe the girl Lusk was an impostor. I thought, as every impartial, cool observer must, that there was a something—not charlatanism—in this matter, and I think, in the end, I got the key to it; but of that you must judge.

The matter puzzled and troubled me so much that I determined to try an experiment, which, perhaps, was cruel. I took Ellen to a medium, without warning her of my intention. Warrick told me of her,—"She has never showed herself in public." He said, "She takes no pay. That makes me trust her. She's miserably poor, too; a huckster in the Cincinnati market."

It was early dawn when I took Ellen to her. She occupied a corner of the market as a fruit and vegetable stall, and as we came near was hanging nets of apples and oranges in front of it, I remember. A skinny, sour-visaged, middle-aged woman, dressed in a sluttish gown and calico sun-bonnet. I noticed the same peculiarity in the eye as in the girl Lusk: they were opaque, gray, dead. The market-house was nearly empty; a few butchers were arranging their meat at some distance inside, or swallowing their coffee at the eating-stalls by the light of a few candles. This woman's stall was out on the solitary street, however, and the pleasant morning light shone about it.

I made a pretence of buying some fruit. "This is the business for which I brought you ashore," I said to Ellen.

It was impossible that the woman could have heard me, yet she turned sharply, eying Ellen as she came forward.

"It was for no oranges you come. Why didn't ye say what you come for? If there's any dead belonging to ye, I'll bring ye word from them. There's spirits all about me; there's spirits at yer back, there's spirits fillin' the street. What'll you have, my young man?" to a boy who stopped. "Eight and ten cents them is."

Ellen drew back. "Let us go, let us go," she said.

At that moment a series of soft double-knocks, as if made by two knuckles of a gloved hand, sounded all about us,—under the pavement, on the roof, on the stall.

"There's yer change.—I've a message for *you*," suddenly facing Ellen; "there's a spirit here to speak to you."

"He is dead, then?" catching both hands together as if to support herself.

The woman took down a greasy card, on which the alphabet was printed, from a nail where it hung, and ran her pencil lightly along it, as the raps continued in swift, soft succession. She spelled out this message:—

"I think of you here. Of you and Joe. You will come to me."

"Where—how was it done?" I cried.

The woman glanced at Ellen, who leaned against the edge of the block.

"I was murdered; drugged and murdered," was the answer.

"He is dead. There is no chance any more." That was all she said, with a strange inconsistency, forgetting her anger of the other day. "There is no chance, no chance," I heard her mutter, as we went back to the boat; "he's gone now."

The blow was as hard as if it had struck her for the first time. I told Warrick the story without comment.

"It goes dead against the other," he exclaimed. "And yet where did either woman get their knowledge of the business we wanted cleared. The blood-mark on the chin, the possibility that the dead man had been drugged and murdered? There's truth in it, in all the muddle."

I said nothing. But the matter had taken a hold on me which I could not shake off. I determined to look through the absurdity and mystery of this so-called spiritualism until I had discovered the truth which Warrick believed lay in it. I could not divest myself, either, of an unaccountable impression that at last we were upon the track of the missing man.

I induced Mrs. Wylie to remain on the boat during its next run, for the boy's sake, who grew stronger and more rugged every day. There was the making of a man in the little fellow; he had a hearty, straightforward look in his puny face, that made a friend of everybody. For the woman, from the day when the message came to her from her husband, dead, she gave way in mind or body as if some sinew had been snapped which had held her up. I fancied that unconsciously she had been keeping some vague hope alive which was gone now, forever. She crept out now to the hurricane-deck, and sat all day; where her look settled, or her hands fell on her lap, there they rested, immovable. As I knew her better, I discovered why the men held her in such a pitying aspect. She was a simple-hearted, credulous creature, such as everybody feels bound and anxious to take care of when they are left drifting about the world.

So we made our way up to the headwaters of the Ohio. It was late in October, I remember,—warm, yellow sunshine by day, and cold nights. The fields nipped brown and red in the early frosts. I used to think if anything could take the poor woman's thoughts off the dead, the cheerful sights and sounds along shore ought to do it. The water was unusually clear, and curdled and bubbled back from the edge of the boat all day, filled with a frothed, green light; the hills on both sides kept rising back and back to the sky beyond, mottled with purple and crimson and blackish greens; we passed thousands of little islands shying out of the current, which were mere beds of feathery moss and golden-rod. Then there were pretty, new little villages, and the busy larger towns, and farms, at long intervals; and when these were passed we floated into the deep solitude again. I noticed it the more because we were out of our usual run; the Strader plied then between Louisville and New Orleans. But the woman saw nothing of it, I think.

When we reached Pittsburg, and had discharged cargo, I determined, with Warrick, to make a final test of the matter. F. was then in the city, just back from England, the most successful medium, next to Home, who ever left the States. He was willing, "for a consideration," to hold a private *séance* and bring us in contact with any of the dead.

He was hardly the person to whom one would think St. Peter would have lent his keys for ever so short a time; an oily, bloated sensualist, with thick lips, and thicker eyelids half closed over a dull, sleepy eye. He was dressed like an Orleans blackleg, gaudy with purple velvet waistcoat and flash jewelry. But if there was any truth in spiritualism, here was its interpreter. I engaged him to come on board on Saturday evening; no one was to be present but Warrick, Ellen, and myself; the boat was empty at the time, with the exception of its regular crew, below. There was but little persuasion needed to induce Ellen to consent.

"He may bring me another message," with a light flickering into her eyes. "Joe will be glad to find the way." It is people like Ellen who are always sure converts of spiritualism; it seems so natural to them that their dead should come back, that they are blind to any absurd discrepancies in the manner. On Saturday morning, on the wharf, I met Stein, who had left the boat some two years before, and remembering his old liking for Joe, told him what we were about to do. Stein was a hard-headed, shrewd little Yankee; I was surprised, therefore, to see how discomposed and startled he appeared at the first mention of the affair; he denounced F. as a humbug with a great deal of heat, and tried to persuade and chaff me out of it; but finding he could not, asked leave to come himself to the *séance*.

"You're bitten, Captain," he said. "It will be easy to persuade you that you see ghosts yourself. You had better let me bring a little daylight with me."

I told Warrick of my meeting with Stein, and he, having nothing else to do, sauntered off in the afternoon to bring him down. I told Ellen also, who, to my surprise, reddened and grew pale, when I named him.

"He is a man whom I have no reason to like," she said. "But it does not matter."

In the evening F. came on board, stopping in the outer cabin, where we were soon joined by Stein. We waited an hour for Warrick, who did not return, and then entered the saloon where Ellen was seated. I noticed that Stein drew back, muttering, "You did not tell me that woman was here," and that no greeting passed between them.

The *séance* proceeded according to the usual formula. We sat around a bare table, on which were placed by Stein and myself the names of those whom we wished to appear written on scraps of paper rolled up in pellets, and laid in a small heap. Ellen wrote none. "He will come," she said, simply.

But few raps were heard. F. delivered the messages by writing, his fat, lumpy hand moving spasmodically over the sheets of paper. From several of the names written on the pellets came communications, vague and meaningless, any one of which might have been exchanged for the other without loss of force.

F. glanced shrewdly around from time to time, fixing his strange, introverted gaze oftenest on Ellen and little Joe, who had crept in and stood looking him boldly in the face. He turned to me.

"One whom you desire to appear has not yet come? So far the *séance* has failed—for you?" he said.

I nodded. His face heightened in color as if the blood slowly rose to his head; the veins swelled; drops of sweat oozed out on his neck and forehead;

he peered sharply about the room, as if out of the dark shadows he expected visible spirits to rise.

"He is coming!" said Ellen, with a gasp. Stein became ghastly pale at the words, and looked, terrified, over his shoulder, recovering himself with a feeble laugh.

The table where we sat was under the chandelier, two of the lamps of which barely sufficed to light that end of the cabin. The remainder stretched, long and narrow and black, to the far upper deck. The medium, looking at Stein as if he saw through him into this outer darkness, sat motionless. There was a long silence. Then he raised his hand, made a slow beckoning movement into the shadow. Ellen and Stein turned their pale faces, breathlessly.

"They are coming! They are here!" he said. "They tell me all you would know. The man you seek is not dead. He was cheated, deceived, carried off to Caraccas that another man might marry his wife."

As his voice rose, Stein rose with it, stood facing him with a look of terror and ferocity, like a wild animal whose lair has suddenly been uncovered. Sudden light flashed on me. I sprang up; Ellen cowered with a cry, but above all sounded F.'s sharp, monotonous sentences.

"He is not dead; he has returned! He is—*here!*" as Stein, with an oath, pointed into the shadow where Warrick appeared, and leaped back as though the ghost of his victim confronted him.

It was no ghost. A little, red-headed, weak-eyed fellow had his arms about Ellen's neck, holding her to his breast as if he had the strength of a lion. Warrick, the medium, and I exclaimed and swore, choking for words; but he was silent. He only held her as close as if he had indeed come back from the grave to find her, putting back her head, now and then, and looking at her with a wonderful love in his puny, insignificant face.

"Ellen! Ellen!" he said at last; "they told me you were dead,—you and the boy. This my Joe!—little Joe?" picking up the boy, handling his legs and arms and looking into his face, his own contorted and wet with tears. We men moved off down into the lower cabin, leaving them alone; but I saw Joe a long time after, still sitting there with his wife clinging to him, and the boy on his knees, and I could not help it, I went in and held out my hand. "I congratulate you, old fellow! God has been good to you!"

But he only looked up with a bewildered smile. "Yes, God has been good. This is Ellen, Captain. And my little son. *My little son.*"

Wylie's story is soon told. Stein had persuaded him to give his creditors the slip and make for California, promising to join him shortly, and that they would speedily make their fortunes. Wylie was a man easily led, and consented. He was concealed under a trap-door in the cigar-shop, and escaped while Fordyce and I sought the police.

Stein had intercepted his letters to his wife until such time as he could send him word of her death. In his own plans upon her he was disappointed.

I am glad to say that Joe brought back enough yellow dust to keep the wolf from the door for many a day. He and his wife are living somewhere in Indiana. Joe, their son, was a drummer-boy in the Thirty-sixth Ohio, under Captain Saunders, and I'll venture to say no braver heart kept time to his "Rat-tat-too" than that which beat under his own little jacket.

I consented to write down these facts, as I said, because of their bearing upon the matter of spiritualism. In this case, as in every other of which I have become cognizant, the mediums have only put into shape the thoughts of those who question them. To admit that certain persons can at will become possessed of the secret movements in the mind of another, will solve the whole mystery. In this case of Wylie, the mediums, Lusk, the woman at Cincinnati, and finally F., simply reproduced the surmises or knowledge of Warrick, Ellen, and Stein. It is not agreeable to think that an animal so gross as F. should have power to decipher our inmost thoughts. Better that, however, than to believe that those we have lost should hold out their hands to us through such a messenger.

FOOTNOTES:

[A] Kant, who carried his demands of unconditional veracity to so extravagant a length as to affirm, that, if a man were to see an innocent person escape from a murderer, it would be his duty, on being questioned by the murderer, to tell the truth, and to point out the retreat of the innocent person, under any certainty of causing murder. Lest this doctrine should be supposed to have escaped him in any heat of dispute, on being taxed with it by a celebrated French writer, he solemnly reaffirmed it, with his reasons.

[B] "June 1, 1675.—Drinke part of 3 boules of punch (a liquor very strainge to me)," says the Rev. Mr. Henry Teonge, in his Diary lately published. In a note on this passage, a reference is made to Fryer's Travels to the East Indies, 1672, who speaks of "that enervating liquor called *Paunch* (which is Indostan for five), from five ingredients." Made thus, it seems the medical men called it Diapente; if with four only, Diatessaron. No doubt, it was its evangelical name that recommended it to the Rev. Mr. Teonge.

9 789362 925688